CREATION

& N   CREATION

A FUTURE
ACTIVITY

JOHN REUMANN

16809

Augsburg Publishing House
Minneapolis, Minnesota

Creation and New Creation

DATE DUE

GAYLORD 234   PRINTED IN U. S. A.

Manufa...

Contents

Preface

Most of the material which follows, in Chapters II-IV, was presented as lectures at the annual Pastors' Institute of St. Olaf College, Northfield, Minnesota, July 24-27, 1972. Chapter I and the conclusions, which time did not allow to be given in full at those lectures, were already drafted at that time, but subsequently reconsidered while revising the entire manuscript during a sabbatical semester, September–December, 1972, spent teaching in the Division of Research and Post-Graduate Studies at the United Theological College, Bangalore, India.

Much of the material in the lectures and hence this book was initially developed in courses and seminars at the Lutheran Theological Seminary, Philadelphia. My interest in the topic has been heightened by current discussions of creation and new creation indicated in the notes to Chapter I, especially in matters of ecology; and specifically by an assignment to produce a brief essay on the topic for the final volume in the four-part series initiated by the Institute for Ecumenical Research, Strasbourg, France (vols. 1 and 2, in English, *The Gospel and Unity* and *The Gospel and Human Destiny* [Minneapolis: Augsburg, 1971]). This essay, scheduled to be published in its German version by Vandenhoeck & Ruprecht, of Göttingen, in 1973, provides the overall, theologically oriented survey of which the present chapters are a popular but more fully detailed analysis of selected biblical passages. There is sufficient material on hand that it is my hope to publish a more thorough

4

treatment for the advanced student and specialist on creation/new creation in biblical and related literatures, organized along "tradition history" lines, in the future.

To President Sidney Rand; Dr. Harlan Foss, head of the Department of Religion; and Dr. Harold Ditmanson, of St. Olaf College, I wish to express my thanks for the invitation to put some of this vast material in a form for public presentation; for their hospitality and for "much good talk," testing ideas, during a delightful stay in Minnesota. To a number of my colleagues in Philadelphia I am indebted for advice and direction, especially in matters outside the normal purview of a New Testament teacher; I must mention with appreciation Drs. Foster R. McCurley Jr., Robert E. Bornemann, Gerhard Krodel, and William Lazareth. In India I experienced many kindnesses from Dr. E. C. John, Acting Principal, and the teaching and library staff at United Theological College, for which *meku tsāla vandanālu*. Dr. Vilmos Vajta, his associates, and the participants in Volume IV of the Strasbourg project, are responsible for pushing me into the topic in a major way and have developed my thinking greatly.

Finally, since no one is what he is in God's creation or as God's creature without basic influences from the homes that touch his life and from the preaching and examples he perceives in formative years, I wish to dedicate these pages to my father and father-in-law, both retired pastors, each over half a century proclaiming grace in God's world, and to my mother-in-law and step-mother, the Rev. and Mrs. W. Paul Reumann, D.D., Lansdale, Pa., and the Rev. and Mrs. Charles F. Brobst, D.D., Telford, Pa. Among other things "in the beginning" for each of us are parents, who as Christians have the challenge to unite the new in Christ with the glories and realities of the world.

JOHN REUMANN

United Theological College
Bangalore 6, South India

I

New Interest
in Creation
and New Creation

The subject of "creation" and its related theme, "the new creation," have in recent years come into fresh and widespread prominence. And for good reasons, which we shall detail below.

The one phrase is directly biblical. "New creation" occurs twice in the letters of Paul and seems to have come into wider use precisely from its New Testament background as a commonplace for something utterly novel and significant — as when Charles Sprague wrote in his "Ode" for the Shakespeare Celebration in Boston in 1823,

> Then Shakespeare arose!
> Across the trembling strings
> His daring hand he flings,
> And lo! a new creation grows!

The other term, "creation," though shared as a concept by the Bible with virtually every religion and philosophy in the world, is a key theme in scripture. Hence we can properly make these two terms the focal points for a study in biblical theology. It is a study, however, which must range over both the testaments, from Genesis to the Revelation of St. John the Divine, and beyond, even if we can pause to examine only selected examples.

At the outset, working definitions are in order as to what we include under each heading. "New creation" is a phrase occurring at Galatians 6:15 and 2 Corinthians 5:17. It conjures up, as Joseph

Sittler has put it, a promise (from God), a faith (in God and self), and a program[1] — as well as, we shall want to add, a people. But just what faith holds about the promise and program of the new creation, for the people of God and for the world, in St. Paul's thought and today, is what is at issue and needs to be discussed.

The other term, "creation," as a recent source book on the impact of this idea insists, is "a part of our day-to-day intellectual baggage" that has to do, not just with "beginnings" of man and the world, but with "the belief that all beings are totally dependent on a transcendent, extratemporal and personal source," i.e., on God as a "radical transcendence," between whom and his creation there is, in Kierkegaard's phrase, "infinite qualitative difference." [2] The anthology on *Creation*, just cited, is subdivided into three parts: Nature, Man, and Society. For our investigation in biblical theology the topic must include also, and above all, God, in addition to man, nature, and society, and under "nature" or some such term must be implied the whole cosmos, inanimate as well as animated — what the Bible calls the "creature" of the Creator. "Creation" thus encompasses what the ancients referred to as "the heavens and the earth and all that is therein," or "mother earth and her children" — what moderns call "brother earth" and "sister nature" [3] — ultimately "the solar system as sibling" of humanity. But how the Bible speaks of these things, and what it means, we must ascertain more clearly.

A. Creation to the Fore

To give reasons why these subjects have leaped into prominence recently is really to recite the factors which agitate much of our contemporary life and thought. The following elements might be briefly listed, however, as illustrative, if not definitive, factors to account for the concern with creation in the late nineteen sixties and the seventies.

(1) To begin with, creation is, of course, a topic of perennial interest, in Christian theology as in religion and philosophy generally. The Apostles' Creed begins,

> I believe in God, the Father Almighty,
> *creator of heaven and earth.*

The Nicene Creed expands the First Article to read,

> We believe in one God, the Father, the Almighty,
> *maker of heaven and earth, of all that is seen and unseen.*[4]

Scarcely a year goes by without some new books or articles on God the creator.[5]

(2) Those very creeds of Christendom just cited reflect within themselves a certain tension between creation and redemption: God the Father creates, God the Son redeems. Creation is mentioned first, but the saving work of Jesus Christ is presented in more detail. The tension referred to has to do with the emphases of the First and Second Articles. To pose it in terms of New Testament passages, is the sequence *"Father, Son* (and Holy Spirit),*"* as Matthew 28:19 and 1 Corinthians 12:4-6 have it, or is it "the grace of our Lord *Jesus Christ* (primary), the love of *God* (seen through Christ's deed), (and participation thereby in the Holy Spirit)," as 2 Corinthians 13:14 arranges it? To put the matter in theological terms, is redemption the center of it all, in light of which we speak about creation, or is creation the starting point, for the sake of which God's acts of redemption take place? We have tensions involving creation and redemption and the roles of God and Christ.

To such questions Christians have given varying answers over the centuries, in the long haul emphasizing redemption and the Second Article more than creation and the First. So it was that Ludwig Feuerbach, who died just over a hundred years ago, could conclude, "Nature, the world, has no value, no interest for Christians. The Christian thinks only of himself and the salvation of his soul." [6] In more recent times such giants as Karl Barth and Rudolf Bultmann and most theologies of "salvation history" have done little to disabuse that idea. But more recently some theologians have elevated creation to new prominence. Creation is, for example, the theme which runs through most of the work of the Swedish systematician, Gustaf Wingren, even if his most recent tour-de-force, which charges that virtually all that is wrong in modern theology is due to a "flight from creation," may be a bit of an "overkill." [7] Yet others share with Wingren this emphasis on creation and have sought to bring creation to our attention theologically.

In the swing of the pendulum which marks so much of the history of theology we must say that in the past decade or so the swing has been toward a new emphasis on creation.

(3) Needless to say, both the perennial interest in creation and the current reemphasis of it derive not merely from theological dynamics but from the very nature of the world in which we live, from the current events of our day and what is happening on "spaceship earth." Two or three examples can serve to pinpoint man's accelerating interest in the world where we "live and move and have our being."

The centenary in 1959 of Charles Darwin's book, *The Origin of Species,* called attention to the rapid march of scientific discovery since the nineteenth century. In that time medical breakthroughs, technological advances, and ventures on the earth, under the sea, into the earth's atmosphere, and into the secrets of the human body and mind have made the world of creation more familiar and more exciting and challenging than ever before. Exploration of outer space has made it possible for man to view his planet, for the first time, literally, from afar and as a unity of which he is but a small part. Thus we have a new vantage point from which to observe human life and activity, and the possibility of new perspectives.

(4) All this new-found knowledge, technology, and achievement, however, threaten to turn to ashes. We attain new industrial goals, putting more cars on bigger and better roads — only to discover we are disastrously polluting the atmosphere and gobbling up the land with strangling ribbons of concrete. We attain higher standards of living — only to find the lake where we want to go during new-found leisure time has become contaminated, and our civilization dying not merely in the glut of "asphalt road and a thousand lost golf balls," [8] but in the refuse of our packaging, garbage, and trash. The ecology crisis of today scarcely needs to be detailed for anyone; it is upon us, in headlines and in a dozen daily annoying and sometimes potentially fatal ways. Must Lake Constance die? Europeans ask. Can the Hudson or the Rhine or the Mississippi be restored to something of what they once were? Even the newspapers of Bangalore mourn the effects from the cutting of the trees, and the dearth of birds because of industrialization in India. All eyes

are on creation, to see whether earth can continue to be a habitable and hospitable home for man. The crisis is that serious.

(5) In all these concerns about ecology and the world we have come to experience a new sort of universality in that we realize we are dealing with common human problems, not confined to Christians or Americans, not limited to one denomination, social strata, or geographical area. These problems touch us all. Wendell Wilkie's "One World" has come true, with a vengeance — one world, it seems, of problems, where we share the dilemmas of creation with all our fellows, passengers or prisoners, on this globe.

Nowhere is this insight truer than when we come to deal with problems of social ethics. Christians can issue statements on matters like racial justice or abortion or divorce. The Lutheran Church in America, for example, with which I am most familiar, can set forth fairly progressive guidelines for members on such issues, but church members must work not merely with other Lutherans or even fellow-Christians to achieve the goals, but with all men of good will, and sometimes people of ill-will, in the world where such goals need to be attained. The Christian of today, interested in implementing in society those things which make for the public good, must work with Protestant, Catholic, and Orthodox believers, Jews of all outlooks, Black Panthers, secularists, atheists, Hindus, Moslems — whatever the populace includes in a pluralistic society. Such a situation suggests that, while our motives in many undertakings may be distinctly Christian, our goals and aims in society will derive from the realm of creation common to all and not merely from the redemptive experience which has been ours in Jesus Christ.

This universality of concern among all men under creation which we find in social matters also applies in "stewardship." In the 1950s and '60s stewardship became a technical term and specific interest of the redeemed Christian. It embraced "what he did with his life after he said 'yes' to Jesus Christ." That sense of Christian stewardship ought not to be lost. But the word stewardship has also begun to be used to describe the role that all men have to exercise within the world that God has given them.[9] It has begun to dawn on us that we need to speak of a stewardship which all men owe, regardless of religious commitment, concerning the world they have inherited, as well as of a stewardship to be practiced by Christians in response to the love they have known from God in Jesus.

All this is to argue that in addition to Christian personal ethics there are also social ethics involving Christians and all persons in the world; a stewardship of creation as well as a Christian steward-ship of redemption. We deal with God's creation as well as with God's new creatures in Jesus Christ as the subject of this book. But again, in this instance too, creation has come to the fore.

B. Creation Theology

The ancient Stoic philosophers, some of whose phrases we shall meet with when we turn to creation in the New Testament, liked to talk of the world as the "house" or "household of God" *(oikos theou,* in Greek). They discussed how everything in this household was arranged providentially, through what they termed the "econ-omy" *(oikonomia),* or providence of God. From this term *oikonomia,* which views the cosmos as a well-organized city-state *(polis)* or household *(oikos),* we get our term "economics," denoting the man-agement of this (cosmic) household, and from it derive the idea of stewardship, for a steward's managing of such a household.[10] In recent theology, terms have begun to be used like "ecological theol-ogy" or "eco-theology" for short, meaning a "theology of nature that takes into account the present ecological crisis-consciousness." [11] The terms are new, but the scope is not, for the ancient Stoics and, I think, some of the Bible's theological writers, also thought in just such broad terms, even though they were not pressured by the same urgency we face today and even if not all Christian theology through the centuries has paid equal attention to the world of creation or nature.

Ecological attitudes over the years have been divided into two types by Frederick Elder, types which stand in sharp contrast. There is (a) the "exclusionist" approach, which emphasizes man *over* his environment and stresses the uniqueness of man-in-*history* as distinct from his environment; and (b) the "inclusionist" ap-proach, which stresses man *in* his environment, and the solidarity of man in *nature* as an integral part of the organic web of life.[12] The former position ties in with what has been termed "the Tertullian Family" [13] in the history of Christian thought, so called from the famous rhetorical question of the second-century church father, Tertullian, who asked,

> What, indeed, has Athens to do with Jerusalem?
> What concord is there between the Academy [of Plato] and the Church? [14]

Tertullianists see no link between the two; Athens, Greek philosophy and wisdom, the world, nature, and the environment are not to be compared with Jerusalem, the Semitic, biblical revelation, history, and "man against his environment." The alternative to Tertullianism has often taken the form of a kind of "Christian Platonism" which admits Athens as well as Jerusalem to the fold, wisdom *and* revelation, nature *and* history, the Academy of Plato *and* the Bible, inclusionistically.

It is conviction of the pages which follow, however, that while the Christian today, simple believer and theologian alike, needs to avail himself of all knowledge about God and the world available both through the natural world, common sense, and science, and through revelation, the biblical position itself is not so exclusivistic as has often been supposed, and that when the full array of biblical positions on creation are explored, there is a grandeur, variety, and breadth which Christian thinking has seldom tapped, regarding creation theology.

Accordingly, one aim of these chapters is to explore a portion of *what* scripture says on creation, and *how* it speaks about it, in an effort to find not only *content* but also *method* for speaking today. The Bible may not be as "exclusionist" as the "family of Tertullian" has supposed, or as "inclusionist" as some modern voices think.

Our contention as to the variety of biblical views of creation has been well put by John Macquarrie in his inaugural lecture as Lady Margaret Professor of Divinity at Oxford.[15] First he set forth the conflicting claims about "the biblical doctrine of creation" and modern Western science and technology. Some, like Harvey Cox and Johannes Metz, have attributed modern progress in the sciences precisely to the "Hebrew understanding of creation" which "separates nature from God" and allows the world to be probed in a matter-of-fact way and thus nature to be available for human use.[16] But others, notably Lynn White, have turned this claim around, so that the Bible is made responsible for "the deterioration of the environment." The point is made in this way. The verses at Genesis 1:26, 28 (where man is commanded to "have dominion" and to subdue the earth"), it is said, have been made the charter for anthropocentric exploitation of the creation, as if the Bible enjoins man's rape of the world.[17]

Macquarrie goes on to give the problem of environment and technology a religious setting by citing the demand of the Marxist philosopher Herbert Marcuse for "a new type of man, a different type of human being, with new needs, capable of finding a qualitatively different way of life, and of constructing a qualitatively different environment." [18] Such a call, Macquarrie holds, amounts to "a religious demand, for a new type of man emerges only where there are fundamentally new evaluations, and these in turn spring from fundamental convictions of a metaphysical or theological kind." [19]

In moving toward his own solution, which turns out to be "organic theism," Macquarrie emphasizes that "the Hebrew tradition" regarding creation really "is a complex one." [20] (One must add that the New Testament tradition makes this complexity even more involved.) Hence in the Old Testament Macquarrie finds more than one model for understanding God and the world, and out of these he chooses a model which is serviceable for needs today. I would agree with his basic contention about the pluralism of ways in which faith speaks in the Bible about God and the world. To explore some of these biblical models concerning creation is the intent of our presentation.

In the remarks just quoted from Professor Macquarrie it will be seen that discussion of the world and its environment immediately involves us also in the question of man. In the view of Lynn White and others, is the anthropocentricity of Genesis 1 the cause of Judeo-Christian "arrogance toward nature"? [21] Is it true that, as a biologist has written in a church study on ecology, "man — in his greed, his desire to conquer nature, his ignorance of this planet as a closed and highly interrelated system, and his failure as caretaker of God's creation — is THE causative factor in the environmental crisis"? [22] If, in Marcuse's words, "a new type of man" is needed, where will he be found?

C. New Creation

That series of questions can serve to introduce us to our other focal term, the "new creation." For this phrase has often been employed to describe a new type of man — the man in Christ — as well as to embrace the dream of a new world. The biblical phrase in Greek, *kainē ktisis,* found at Galatians 6:15 and 2 Corinthians 5:17, can be translated either as "new creature" or "new creation" — that is, it can refer either to a new kind of individual or to a renovated cosmos. As we shall see in Chapter IV, that difference in translation is precisely a point at issue in interpreting Paul. For the time being, recognizing both meanings as possible, we shall simply list some factors which have caused the "new creation" to become a prominent theme in our day.

(1) The idea of the individual Christian as "a being created anew" has been stressed repeatedly by Rudolf Bultmann, among others, in interpreting the thought of Paul. In Bultmann's hands, the verse at 2 Corinthians 5:16f., which denigrates the "Christ after the flesh" (interpreted to mean the historical Jesus) and rejoices in that "eschatological occurrence through the proclaimed word" that produces "existence in faith" for the "new creature in Christ," has been made an interpretative key for Paul and for theology generally.[23] On the homiletical and theological levels the writings of Paul Tillich, particularly his sermons, about the "new being," have popularized and deepened this existential understanding.[24]

(2) The notion of the new creation as a better world to come has been so pervasive that it scarcely requires documenting. Sometimes this sort of new creation has been expected to come apocalyptically; such a view has been espoused especially in sect groups and among Bible literalists and Pentecostalists. But at times this world-to-come has been identified with the fruit of human effort (as in the period of Liberal theology); or it is said to come through evangelistic effort, or via technology, or by means of some human

device like the United Nations—such effort could bring the new age. More often it has been a vaguer dream that is invoked under the banner of this term, but with political overtones—compare Martin Luther King's phrase, "I have a dream . . ." or the theme employed by the World Council of Churches at Uppsala in 1968, around the phrases from Revelation 21:5, "Behold, I make all things new." [25]

(3) This dream of a better world has more recently become overtly political in that it is to be brought about, in the opinion of some, by political action, revolution, and even bloodshed; compare discussion over the World Conference on Church and Society, Geneva, 1966, sponsored by the World Council of Churches, and the controversy triggered by subsequent grants through the World Council to revolutionary groups in Africa, though for humanitarian purposes. The issue of "evolution or revolution," as the means for achieving the new creation, therefore enters into many discussions about the new creation.

(4) Since, as we shall see, "new creation" has possible roots in apocalyptic thought, revival of interest in that strange world of visions and revelations about the "last things" which we term apocalyptic has been a factor in heightening interest in our theme. Not only sectarian groups which long traded in apocalyptic, but now biblical scholars, theologians, and main-line denominations, who have sought to study and understand it as a fruitful force in Christian origins and for today, have made apocalyptic a living thing.[26] It may be added that at times these ideas of apocalyptic, revolution, and ecology are combined,[27] making "new creation" an even more potent and prominent slogan.

D. Some Difficulties in These Themes

Admittedly, such a theme as new creation presents certain hazards. In addition to the antithesis posed between individual and world as points of emphasis and the matter of evolution or revolution, new creation raises the question whether the goal is to be achieved by man's inventions or God's condescensions, by the human race or divine grace; is the new world to come via technology or theology? through IBM or IHS? Nonetheless, for all the shifts in meaning which the phrase has undergone and all the uncertainties about what exactly it means, new creation is, Joseph Sittler insists, "inevitably the right image" [28] for our day. That being so, our concern is all the more imperative, to inquire what Paul may have meant by it, to guide our current usage.

With the theme of creation there are hidden hazards too. We can run afoul of the old battles of science versus religion, or the whole question of "revelation — what is it?" or the problem of myth, to say nothing of the problem of how we can still talk about God as a meaningful entity today. The relationship of nature to history has already been noted; considerable battles have been fought in Old Testament scholarship over the place of each in Israel's thought. The connection between apocalyptic and nature also enters in.

Two particular problems in dealing with creation need special mention. One has to do with compartmentalization in Christian thinking, or the danger of the "pigeon-hole mentality." It is a common tendency, stemming from the Apostles' and Nicene Creeds themselves, to confine creation to the province of God the Father (Article One) while Jesus Christ is assigned redemption (Article Two). The fact of the matter is that the Bible, more often than not, sees God the Father ("Yahweh" in the Hebrew scriptures) as the One who redeems (this continues true in the New Testament), and Jesus Christ in the writings of the early church plays a role in creation. Thus, our traditional compartments will not do; the biblical evidence bursts the bonds of these neat classifications or pigeon holes.

A more serious matter is the relationship between creation and redemption, a topic already hinted at. To be specific, while many see redemption (and history) as central in the Bible, a few have argued that creation (and thus nature) is a major or even central theme. And some would suggest a reciprocal relationship between the two. Letting "C" stand for creation and "R" redemption,[29] shall we then adopt a basic outlook where the latter is dominant, expressed in the formula $\dfrac{R}{C}$? Or is the former basic, i.e., $\dfrac{C}{R}$? Or do we use a formula with the two in tandem (C/R)? Or do we want to place the two in opposition as the second-century thinker and heretic Marcion did, C versus R? The problem of this relationship we shall find reflected in much literature on Israel's thought and on Pauline theology.

In the few pages of this book we cannot hope to solve all such problems or even touch on them, but we need to be aware of the hazards in handling these topics, as well as why they have come to the fore. Our concern is to view something of the variety of biblical views on creation/new creation, in the hope that the content and models may be suggestive for our day, when the call is to reaffirm "the biblical understanding of creation" and redefine some of "the values by which Christians live" in God's changing world.[30]

E. Outlining an Approach

In the pages of the following chapters we shall ask first, in Chapter II, how faith has spoken about creation in the Bible. Here our examples will be drawn from earliest Christianity, even prior to Paul, and from some of the oldest traditions of Israel, in Genesis 2. Briefer reference will also be made to other examples, notably Colossians 1.

Chapter III will deal with how, for the Bible, creation was not just a one-time thing but is ongoing—in a phrase, "creation continues." Here we shall have to ask what is the relation of this continuing creation by God to what we call redemption. The writings of the greatest prophet during Israel's exile in Babylon, the so-called Second Isaiah, will provide the examples here, against the background of what earlier prophets and priest-poets had said and sung about creation.

Chapter IV will take up Paul's phrase about the new creation. In exploring its meaning we shall have to pay attention to Paul's views on the man in Christ, the church, and baptism, and, as a possible background and setting, the whole sweep of apocalyptic, from the successors of Deutero-Isaiah to the seer of the New Testament apocalypse, especially as he expressed himself in Revelation 21.

Only after that can we hope to pull together in Chapter V some concluding observations from each section as to what the Bible means by creation and new creation. It is hoped that these findings will provide us with a few basic guidelines as to what God's people need to hold fast to, if they are to be loyal to the teachings and vision of scripture, as well as what they may in good conscience let rest a bit more loosely. Along with such clues as to substance, we may also get some methodological insights as to how Israel, old and new, went about making its statements and committing itself on creation. Here may arise some hints as to how we today and our children, in a changing universe, may engage in the same process of speaking about creation, as ongoing affirmation of that "radical transcendence," God, whom we have come to know especially in Jesus Christ.

God's people have not always in the past bled for the right issues or taken a stand at the proper or even strategic points in the terrain of creation. The future may call upon us to make decisions and commit ourselves, together with other persons on earth, as never before, in a self-effacing, interest-sacrificing way, reflecting the biblical image of the servant who suffers for what he stands for. In time to come, being "salt of the earth" and "light of the world" (Matt. 5:13f.) may take on new meanings. Values and life styles may have to be redefined. But the first step, before "reaffirming the biblical understanding of creation," is to find out more about what this understanding is, in the various biblical theologies of Creator and creature.

II

Faith
Speaks about
Creation

How does the Bible speak about creation?

Since creation has to do not merely with origins and "how things came to be the way they are," but also implies in the Bible the dependence of all beings on a "transcendent, ... personal source" [1] — i.e., God the creator is involved — Bible-talk about creation inevitably consists of statements of faith. That, in a nutshell, is what this chapter is about: how the Bible takes the "accepted scientific facts" of its day and uses them to make statements of faith about God, the world, and man.

Such a process we can plainly see when we deal with a creed. For example, "I believe that God has created me and all that exists ..." (Luther's Explanation to the First Article of the Apostles' Creed) is surely an affirmation of faith. We can also see the point when we sing a hymn:

Let the whole creation cry,
"Glory to the Lord on high," (Stopford A. Brooke)

or

God who madest earth and heaven ...
Who the day and night hast given ...
Praise to thee my soul shall render,
        (Heinrich Albert, translated by Catherine Winkworth)

or

19

O Christ, our King, Creator, Lord . . .
Now to our praises bend thine ear,
                    (St. Gregory, translated by Ray Palmer)

or, from Ceylon,

Word of the Father, by whom was creation,
Word become flesh, Thou hast wrought man's salvation,
Jesus, to Thee glory be: Jesus to Thee (D. T. Niles).[2]

In all these instances we hear the language of praise and confession. But when we read a description of creation in the Bible, we do not always realize that here, too, it is faith speaking. Yet because the statement is about God and what he has done, it must be a matter of faith; the faith of Israel or of the Christian community is expressing itself. How this works out in Genesis and Paul's letters is the concern of this chapter.

We may begin by calling attention to the amazing number and variety of views which exist in the Bible concerning creation. More than fifteen different "creation theologies" in the Old and New Testaments can be identified, to say nothing of variations which appear in the literature of the Intertestamental Period outside the usual canon. There is, for example, the view of creation found in the Priestly writer in Genesis 1 and 5, which is different from the view of the Yahwist in Genesis 2 and 3. There is the sort of "Zion-theology" [3] present especially in some of the Psalms, which touches on creation in its own way. We have reflections about creation in the prophets and the wisdom literature, two categories which can be broken down into even more specific components, such as the view in the Book of Amos, or in Jeremiah, or in Job and Proverbs, among others. The distinctive use of creation imagery by Deutero-Isaiah we shall explore in Chapter III. There is also the further view of Third Isaiah and the apocalyptists. In the New Testament we have material from Paul and John, from apocalyptic writers and the pre-Pauline Hellenistic church, plus Jesus and the Deutero-Paulines. In all these cases there are distinct and differing views of creation, spread over a thousand-year period, each nuanced in its own way.

These varying manners in which biblical faith saw creation, I once outlined for a group of theologians, some of whom had championed creation as a theme in their own work as systematicians. It was surprising to discover their negative reaction to such variety. "Where is '*the* biblical doctrine of creation'?" they asked. The fact of the matter is that "the biblical doctrine" is often a simplified composite — or even, in the hands of some, an ideology — which, in putting together the Bible's pluralistic statements on a topic, tends to overlook certain aspects or to underplay some parts of scripture.

In recent biblical studies, however, a tradition-history approach has been emerging which encourages us to place these many biblical statements of faith in the sequence in which they developed (insofar as we can tell this). "The biblical doctrine" thus becomes a series of statements of faith in differing situations over the centuries, about which we must make decisions concerning what is normative and what is useful today.

Sometimes, to be sure, we can sense common threads running through all of these statements, but sometimes we must simply let the paradoxical variety stand in tension: the Bible includes both this and that. There is also usually a further history, over some nineteen hundred subsequent years, of how Christian faith within the church has expressed itself on such issues, sometimes repeating, sometimes recasting, sometimes reworking or even repudiating elements in this earlier witness. Church history and the history of doctrine have the task of recounting these later statements. Systematic theology then has the opportunity of taking all this witness and traditions and reinterpretations and reiterating its truths that are pertinent to the day, in the language of the times.

The average Christian, of course, has the option of repeating the truths of faith in language of the first or fourth or sixteenth century or of our 1970s or the 970s B.C., but the systematician has the challenge constantly of exploring new frontiers. At times the church (or some portion of it) may pick out, for historical or theological reasons, some particular statement of faith as having preeminence, or it can, as part of confessional theology, elevate some article of faith as norm.[4] These confessional statements have their place, and it is often a key one in biblical interpretation. Scriptural loyalty puts a fence, as it were, around a particular collection of documents of faith, the canon; these are regarded as regulative. Historical study treats these documents, often together with related ones out-side the canon, so as to elucidate the meaning of author and original audience. A theological approach reserves the right to judge the content of each statement in the scriptures by the heart of scripture, the gospel of Jesus Christ (or whatever else has been decided upon as criterion). And to ascertain the gospel criterion, later creeds can serve as pointers.

In these last three paragraphs I have, of course, been setting forth, in brief, what might be called an evangelical hermeneutic, which provides a way of living with, and profiting from, the history of and variety within scripture and its interpretations over the years. It is a way of saying where we "put our money" amid the many options open for the use of scripture nowadays. The method, to repeat, means attention to the historical development of the biblical witnesses and their later extension in the church, recog-nizing the existence of all strands and singling out certain of them as master themes to which the church must hold true, either be-cause of their perdurance or obvious centrality in the biblical records. Implied also is our learning from the whole process how faith has spoken in the past, so that it may find expression in our day too.

But to return to the particular point from which our hermeneutic began: there exist in the Bible an amazing variety and number of statements on creation. Three decades or so ago it was fashionable to stress the unity of this biblical witness. Today the style is to emphasize the pluralism or variety.[5] I have no doubt but that in time those who care for holy scripture will return to a stress on unity, when the pendulum swings again. But for the present we can rejoice in the variety — it gives us ever so many more ways of speaking, and offers leads for doing theology today in a time of change. *E Pluribus unum*, "one out of many," is a good motto in United States history and a noble goal in theology; however, right now the mood is *de pluribus*, pluralism.

Before we turn to passages where faith speaks about creation in the Bible, however, there is a second current trend which deserves to be mentioned, even if more briefly. That is the tendency to place biblical statements about creation squarely within their con-text in the history of religions generally. For the Old Testament's plethora of creation theologies, that means setting each in relation to non-Israelite creation legends, stories, and theologies, from Egypt, Mesopotamia, Ugarit and the Canaanites, and later from Greece and Persia.[6] For the New Testament, attention to Intertestamental developments is called for, as well as to Greek, Hellenistic, Ptolemaic, Stoic, and other views, and ideas in the mystery cults, to mention only a few of the categories of nations, eras, cultures, philosophies, and religions that are pertinent.

Such interest in peoples and ideas that were alive in the period during and before which a biblical author wrote, in lands contiguous to Palestine is, of course, but a reflection of sound historical method. If Goethe once rightly said,

> He who would the poet know
> To the poet's land must go,

then the obvious extension is to visit also places that touched in some way the poet's landscape. We live in a time when the universalism of our age encourages attention to all of what proves to be one world. Common sense dictates awareness of more than the narrow boundaries of what we have under specific study. But this history-of-religion approach must be undertaken not only to pile up sources for, and analogues to, the biblical writer, but also to help us see what is unusual about his words and where he speaks against his environment, as well as where he expresses himself in light of it.

To put this second, preliminary emphasis as clearly as possible: No matter how high an understanding of Yahweh's revelation or of the uniqueness of Jesus Christ we may have, no interpreter can fully understand scripture without entering into the most careful analysis possible of the world of the time of that revelation. How the history-of-religion approach works and is pertinent to biblical material will be suggested below, in analyzing certain biblical texts.

Having observed that proper biblical interpretation involves seeing each passage in the course of its development, against the background of the day, we now turn to our two particular examples of faith speaking about creation in the Bible. Ideally, of course, in discussing "the beginning" we should begin at the beginning and

trace through every one of Israel's creation theologies in chrono-
logical sequence, followed by the examples from the Intertestamental Period, and then the New Testament statements. Space will
not permit such detail here, and so we choose two striking examples
as exhibits A and B from the earliest times of primitive Christian
and ancient Israelite faith.

A. An Early Christian Credo about Christ and Creation

In the year A.D. 54 the apostle Paul was engaged in protracted
correspondence with the Christian congregation at Corinth of which
he was the founding father. The Corinthians had written their
absent apostle a letter raising several questions which had come
up in daily life as they tried to be followers of Jesus Christ in a
cosmopolitan city. One question had to do with what foods, particularly meat, a believer could in good conscience eat (1 Cor. 8:1).[7]
This was a problem because most meat available had either been
part of a sacrifice in a pagan temple and was tainted in the minds
of some by dedication to an idol, or was prepared by a kosher
(Jewish) butcher and bore the stamp of Jewish food laws and
ritual. What should a Christian do?

In sketching his answer (which amounted to saying that a Christian is free to eat whatever he chooses, though he will curb some
of his freedom for the sake of the brother who is weaker in faith),
Paul, in passing, at 1 Corinthians 10:26 makes a statement that is
amazing in its scope for a converted Pharisee just a quarter of a
century after Jesus' death. To undergird his point that the Corinthians are free to eat what is sold at the local meat market (which
was run by pagans) Paul offers as a reason for this freedom the
fact that "the earth is the Lord's, and everything in it" (10:26). All
the earth and its products belong to the Lord.

What is surprising is that Paul here quotes an Old Testament
verse as proof text from Psalm 24:1. Originally that verse had referred to the God of Israel: "the earth is the Lord's, and the fulness
thereof." But Paul seems to apply the term "lord" to Jesus Christ—
he is creator of all, to whom this world belongs, who declares all
things clean.[8] Paul seems also to have deliberately taken a verse
which Judaism of the day employed to reinforce its demand that

a blessing must be spoken over all foods, and to have used it in a most nonlegalistic way: to document freedom from the law.[9] But amazingly, the claim of Christ's lordship over the world, as creator, seems to have been well enough known in the church at Corinth in the year 54 for Paul to make this allusion without further explanation.

That this was so, and that faith in Christ's role in creation goes back even prior to Paul and his preaching in Corinth, are demonstrated by the chief passage to which we turn in 1 Corinthians 8:5-6.

To grasp the context, we must review the Corinthian situation which Paul addresses. Some of his converts in Corinth were Jews, won out of the synagogue where Crispus had been ruler. Others were Gentiles who had been on the fringe of the Jewish faith. Still others must have been won from the pagan world—the Greek religions and philosophies, the mystery cults, the gnostic environment. These baptized brothers and sisters, in seeking to apply their faith, soon came to the problem of what foods to eat, at their fellowship meals with each other and at banquets to which old friends might invite them, of social clubs and guilds, held usually at pagan temples.

It was a question of whether to eat meat that had taken on religious significance by being sacrificed first to some pagan god at the local temple. Christians of Jewish background or influenced by the Hebrew scriptures avoided such idol meats, for the sacrifice had been offered to an idol and henceforth bore his stamp. Gentile Christians and those like Paul who found new freedom in Christ thought nothing of eating such meat. They appealed to the common-sense position that "an idol has no real existence" (8:4) and to the Jewish slogan, "There is no God but one" (8:4b).

Paul tends to agree with the "freedom party": there are no other real gods, only so-called ones, and we are free to eat, but he cautioned that "this liberty of yours" can cause weaker brethren to stumble (8:9). At the very outset of chapter 8 he sets forth the two criteria which will dominate all the discussion through chapter 11: (a) the first criterion is love (8:1ff.), for God, taking the form of concern for the brother for whom Christ died 8:11); and (b) the other is edification, or development, of the community — 8:1, what builds up or edifies the Christian church matters, not what tears it down. The answer must be freedom, but limited by love for the brother and for the community.

Chapter 8 is really a battle of slogans from the various viewpoints being heard, and vv. 5-6 belong to this collection of mottos and creeds. The claim in v. 1, "all of us possess knowledge [in Greek, *gnōsis*]," comes from one group in Corinth which stressed the divine enlightenment its members had. Paul later had to warn that not all, even of those who supposed they did, actually possessed of such knowledge (v. 7). If we ask what such knowledge included, the answer is, according to v. 4, awareness that there is no God but one.

That phrase in v. 4 represents the heart of ancient Israel's creed: Deuteronomy 6:4, "The Lord our God is one Lord." This faith of the *Shema* (so called from the initial word at Deuteronomy 6:4 in Hebrew, "Hear [*shema*], O Israel . . .") is echoed by Jesus at Mark 12:29, "The first commandment of all is this, 'The Lord our God, the Lord, is one.'"

In explicating this Old Testament credo from Deuteronomy, Paul then goes on in vv. 5-6 to provide a lucid insight into how early Christians thought about God and Christ. "For even if there are many so-called gods in heaven or in earth—as indeed there are many 'gods' and many 'lords'. . ." (Paul seems, at least so far as his audience goes, to have reckoned with a host of powers and forces that serve as God in the lives of men, even though these are only "so-called" gods), v. 6 goes on, "yet for us

there is one God, the Father

from whom are all things and for whom we exist,

and one Lord, Jesus Christ,

through whom are all things and through whom we exist."

We pass over the details about how v. 5 reflects Old Testament phrases from Psalm 82:1, 6 (describing Yahweh "in the midst of 'the gods'") and Deuteronomy 10:17 ("the Lord your God is God of gods and Lord of lords"), in order to concentrate on v. 6, which has been widely recognized as a pre-Pauline fragment which Paul quotes and as one of Christendom's oldest statements of faith.

This creed from the Hellenistic Jewish church—for that is what it seems to be—is marked by parallelism, balance, rhythm, and its careful construction. Add the words as a preface "We believe in . . ." and you have a creed of four lines, numbers one and three balancing each other, and two and four modifying them. This can best be seen if we take the words "for us there is . . ." as introducing a Christian confession,

and line one to consist of "one God, the Father,"

modified by line two, "from whom all things are and for whom we exist";

line three, balancing one: "and one Lord, Jesus Christ,"

modified by a fourth line corresponding to two: "through whom all things are and through whom we exist."

Technically this creed is "binitarian"[10] (as distinct from "trinitarian"), for it deals with two persons, the Father and the Son. Its aim must have been polemical; at least here it is employed to exclude other gods: *"for us* there is one God . . . and one Lord, Jesus Christ." What amazes us is the fact that Jesus of Nazareth, the Christ, crucified and risen, is given a place parallel to God and a role in world's creation and preservation. How could all this arise within three decades of Jesus' ministry in Palestine, that he is designated agent in the creation?

There are good grounds for speculating how this particular creed about creation and Christ's lordship took shape, and we can clearly identify some of the building blocks which went into it. The starting point surely was the Jewish-Old Testament confession "God is one"; the Greek employed in v. 6 for "one God" *(heis theos)* is, as we have seen, a standard acclamation, perhaps the most concentrated way of expressing in a single phrase the basic monotheistic faith of Israel.[11] It is a phrase which Paul himself quotes at Galatians 3:20 and Romans 3:30, not to mention 1 Corinthians 8:4.

To that slogan "one God" has been added the phrase in line two, "from whom all things are and for whom we exist." It sounds liturgical and could have been added in synagogue worship, but history-of-religions research enables us to pinpoint the closest analogues to such language. The phrase is Stoic, in sound and content.[12] The later Roman emperor, Marcus Aurelius (A.D. 121-180), a Stoic in philosophy and outlook, employs an almost exactly identical phrase about Nature: "Of you are all things, in you are all things, for you are all things."[13] With it may be compared Romans 11:36, where Paul uses similar stoicizing language about God: "from him and through him and to him are all things." By this phrase the one God, Yahweh, is related to the created world which men of the day, in both Greco-Roman Stoicism and the Jewish synagogue, knew by experience and philosophized about.

We must now make a fresh start with line three. Here, too, we have a formula of acclamation, but this time one used not by Jews but solely by early Christians in acclaiming Jesus Christ as Lord. The words in Greek *kyrios Iēsous Christos* are precisely those employed by early Greek-speaking Christians to hail their master: "Jesus is Lord" (1 Cor. 12:3) or "Jesus Christ is Lord" (Phil. 2:11).[14] Anyone full of the Spirit might break out in just such a cry in the Sunday gathering at Corinth. Jesus is thus confessed as Lord, though not yet as God.

Somewhere, however, in primitive Christianity, probably before the year A.D. 50, some fervent believer put this cry of the believing heart, "Jesus Christ Kyrios" (or Lord) alongside the acclamation of the synagogue which Christians accepted, "one God, from whom all things and for whom we exist." Once that occurred, three steps followed rapidly to make the parallelism complete, as we now have it in v. 6:

a) to balance the phrase "one God," the cardinal number "one" was added in line three, yielding our existing text, "*one* Lord Jesus Christ";

b) to balance that full phrase "(one) Lord Jesus Christ," a title was after "one God" *(heis theos);* to make the parallelism complete, "one God *the Father*" was now confessed. Yahweh had, of course, been called "Father" long before. The intent here may be to designate him as "the Father of our Lord Jesus Christ" (cf. 1 Cor. 1:3). It is also possible that the phrase in this context means "Father of creation or of the universe." [15]

c) Last of all a fourth line was added about Jesus to balance the Stoic description of God the Father. Jesus was said to be the one "through whom are all things [*ta panta*, the Greek suggests 'all creation'], and we exist through him" (the reference is to us Christians; we are the ones who exist in and through Christ). Again, Stoic influence could be claimed, as in line two, but Jewish background is more likely in that wisdom had earlier been viewed by Jews as God's agent in creation; cf. Proverbs 8:22ff. And Jesus Christ was sometimes identified by Christians as the "wisdom of

God" (1 Cor. 1:24). What wisdom was said by Jews to have been in creation, Jesus Christ is now confessed to be.[16] Thus, by the year 50, Jesus has been given a place in the making of all things, as agent of creation, the one through whom we exist. That means he was thought of as preexistent (before the world) and existing for always (beyond us).

It was in some such way as sketched above that this early Christian creed, giving Christ a place in creation and its continuance, took shape, so that Paul could almost casually allude to it in his discussion with the Corinthians on idol meats in A.D. 54. He can agree with them that there is but one God. But note, he goes on, who this God and this Lord of ours are: God the Father, creator of all and judge of Israel (10:1ff.), our creator and judge as well (8:6); Christ who died for the brother who is weak in faith (8:11) and for all of us (15:3), who was God's mediator in bringing all things into being and who sustains his creation (8:6).

There is, of course, much more which might be said about this creation creed, how it is logically arranged and universal in its scope; how it, strikingly, speaks of Christ's work without mentioning the cross or resurrection; and how it assumes a functional unity of Christ with God. One might also play with the prepositions in lines two and four ("from ... for ... , through ... through ..."), a fascinating exercise,[17] reminding one of what Abelard has done in one of his hymns about the Trinity:

> Low before him with our praise we fall,
> *Of* whom, and *in* whom, and *through* whom are all;
> *Of* whom, the Father; and *in* whom, the Son;
> *Through* whom, the Spirit, with them ever one.[18]

But that example simply reminds us of the purpose of such language: not simply to define God dogmatically but to praise him. Confession of faith is doxological.

It is now possible to draw out some findings from this exploration of what is perhaps the earliest Christian creation creed, at 1 Corinthians 8:6.[19] (1) The first thing to strike us is that when this passage speaks of creation, it is in the language of confession: "for us there is ... ," *credimus,* "we believe." This is the redeemed community

speaking. (2) This statement of faith derives much of its expression
and content from the world of the day. We have spotted Stoic
language, Old Testament phrases, Jewish, and Hellenistic ideas.
Faith speaks in the tongues of men. (3) This credo, in spite of its
Stoic-sounding lines, seems to speak not in metaphysical or ontological terms,[20] about the "is"-ness of God but existentially and
even anthropologically, in terms of man. It is a confession *for* us;
we human beings are *from* God and *for* God, and we believers exist
through Christ. Lines two and four conclude on the note of human
existence, under God and Christ.

(4) Obviously of import is the fact that our pre-Pauline formula
involves both God and Christ; each shares in creation and its continuance for us, the Father as source and goal ("of whom ... and
for whom we and all things are") and the Son as agent of creation
and redemption ("through whom ..." in both instances). If the
verse must be analyzed in terms of creation and redemption, then
both God and Christ participate in each activity. Already by the
year A.D. 50 or so, faith had perceived Jesus to be so significant
that a place had to be found for him in all the work of God, including creation. But God is not limited to beginnings; he is the one
"for whom we [Christians] live," as the New American Bible puts it.

(5) More speculatively, it may be possible to ask whether, within
both the realms of creation and redemption, in the world and in
the church, this formula does not see Christians as holding a particular place eschatologically in God's plan. All things — the whole
cosmos of creation — are said to be from God, through the agency
of the Son. But we, we Christians — the word here, *hēmeis*, I take to
refer to those believers in the lordship of Jesus Christ who make
this confession — we live for God and through Christ eschatologically. John Gibbs has ventured the opinion that under the lordship
of Christ Christians are here told to live redemptively, permeating
all things *(ta panta)*, until "the time when all things, as well as
Christians, are *eis auton* [for God]." [21] That notion depends, at
least in part, on how we interpret Romans 8:18-25, about the dependence of the whole creation on the "glorious liberty of the
children of God," to be discussed in Chapter IV. For the present
we may suggest that Christians, according to 1 Corinthians 8:6,
may be meant to have such a role in the world as Matthew envisions

when he talks of disciples as "salt for the earth" and "light of the world," permeating God's creation with the newness of experience and insight which they have come to know in Jesus Christ.

B. Israel Speaks about Creation in a Secularized, Humanistic Age

For our other major example we now must transport ourselves back some ten centuries in time from 1 Corinthians to the monarchy of Israel, when Solomon ruled over a united kingdom, between 961 and 922 B.C. Our interest here is in what a great creative theologian said about creation, in a witness we have in the second chapter of Genesis. The name of this theologian we do not know; conventionally he is called the J writer or "Yahwist," but he is identifiable not merely from the Hebrew term he employs for God (*YHWH*, commonly put into English as "Yahweh") but by dozens of features of style, terminology, idiom, and above all characteristic emphases in thought. When we set this theologian in his times, we cannot but be impressed with his achievement and may even find his way of working appropriate to our day.[22]

We need not spend much time talking about this J source or writer in contrast to the so-called Priestly source. The Priestly writer, P, has given us Genesis 1 and 5 and other segments of the Old Testament; J is responsible for Genesis 2:4b to 4:26 and other portions of the Pentateuch. Grounds for identifying each source have been set forth for a hundred years or so; recently, Norman Habel, in the volume *Literary Criticism of the Old Testament,* in the series "Guides to Biblical Scholarship" has admirably summed up the distinguishing features of Genesis 1 and 2.[23]

In general, P speaks solemnly and majestically, with stereotyped idioms, like "These are the generations of . . ." or "God blessed and said. . . ."; he appeals to the intellect. J is an artist, using the story form, picturesquely and dramatically; he appeals to the imagination. The two may use different Hebrew words for the same idea: *bara'* ("create") in chapter 1, *yasar* ("form") in chapter 2. The Hebrew word *ha'adam*, P uses for "mankind"; J, for "the first man, Adam." Chapter 1, by P, presents a cosmic perspective, God transcendent, creating by fiat, through his mighty word; chapter 2, from J, has a man-centered perspective, God is immanent; creation is, so to speak, by hand — God "forms" (2:7), "breathes into" (2:7*b*), and "plants" a garden (2:8), like an artisan potter or gardener.

In the two accounts the sequence of creation events is quite different, though mankind occupies primacy of place in each. In chapter 1 there is an ascending order of creating throughout six days, till as a climax "God created man in his own image ... male and female he created them" (1:27). In chapter 2 the man is created right off the bat; then comes the garden, trees, cattle, beasts, and birds, and only then, as the suitable helpmate, woman. Genesis 1 rises in a six-stage crescendo; the second chapter is like a circle or a clockface, with man formed at 12 o'clock noon and then after the hand of God traverses the full 360 degrees, woman is brought forth when the hand is at twelve again — not an ascending or descending order, but man and woman are co-equals at the top of the clock. To change the figure, in Benno Jacob's phrase, male and female in chapter 1 are the pinnacle of a pyramid, in chapter 2 the man and the woman are the center of a circle.[24]

Even the opponents, those persons or ideas against whom these chapters were written — and I assume that most biblical passages, certainly most affirmations of faith, were directed against some opposing view or had a particular purpose in a specific situation — even the targets of polemic differ in chapters 1 and 2. For P, the enemy is pagan myth, with its astral deities of sun, moon, and stars (the "heavenly host") and the notion of chaos and powers of disorder; for J, fertility cults in Canaan, perhaps specifically the issue of serpent worship, were the menace.

But we need not here detail any further the case for accepting Genesis 2:4*b* ff. as originally the work of J. More important is the fact that this author of chapter 2 was a loyal worshiper of Yahweh, living about 950 B.C., in the changing world of Solomon's Jerusalem. Eissfeldt has called his work the "Layman's Source" (*Laienschrift*),[25] in contrast to the Priestly document which was finally put together some five hundred years later. Such a conjecture does not add much to our knowledge about the author, but attribution to the Yahwist of a layman's outlook does fit the general picture we shall paint, at least as compared with the priestly outlook developing at the Jerusalem temple of the day. He was clearly not a priest at Solomon's temple, or a leader in its growing cult life, which increasingly seems to have aped practices of pagan temples.

The content of Genesis 2 is so familiar that we need not review it here, but before analyzing it, we do well to remind ourselves that Israel, already in the tenth century B.C., at the outset of its existence as a monarchy, was totally surrounded by creation legends which abounded in the ancient Near East. All of Israel's neighbors had abundant stories of how the world and man began, many of these myths far older, by a millenium or more, than the little group which called itself the "children of Israel" *(bene Israel)* and their creation stories.

In Egypt, for example, where Israel's ancestors had lived in captivity, until the exodus some three centuries before, there were creation accounts to be heard at four major temple centers. That at Heliopolis was about a "watery chaos," out of which the world came; that at Memphis dealt with creation by the divine word of the god Ptah; that at Hermopolis, with the "cosmic egg"; and at Thebes there was a priestly account also, to say nothing of Pharaoh Amen-hotep's monotheistic creation account in his "Hymn to the Sun." [26] In Mesopotamia, whence Abraham was said to have emigrated, Sumerian myths in the millenium between 3000 and 2000 B.C., told of Enlil or Enki as creators,[27] and the later Akkadian epic on creation, the *Enuma elish,* with its battle between Marduk and the forces of chaos, had achieved a place of dominance throughout the Near East.[28] In Ugarit and apparently among Canaanite neighbors, too, there were myths about creation struggles.[29]

The Israelites no doubt reacted to these widespread creation stories in both positive and negative manners. Like their neighbors, they too wanted to speak of the beginnings and attribute to their God a role in creation. Sometimes, however, there must have been voices of opposition to these pagan views and more particularly to the worship practices which they brought with them. Some of the later prophets have been interpreted as making just such protests, and there are scholars who think the so-called E or Elohist source in the Northern Kingdom deliberately left out any creation account, in order to avoid such foreign infiltration of creation ideas as inimicable to Israel's traditional theology. But sometimes, as at points in Genesis 2, portions of ancient Near Eastern creation accounts were adopted and adapted, purified, revised, and thus made compatible with faith in Yahweh. And at times creation material from Israel's neighbors was taken over, virtually intact, and used in praise of Yahweh. Interesting examples of this last-mentioned tendency occur at Genesis 14:19 and 22, where we have what is perhaps the oldest reference in the Bible to creation in the phrase "God most High, Maker of heaven and earth" (but the words, including the name *El-Elyon*, "God most High," give indication of Canaanite origin);[30] and Psalm 104, which parallels Amen-hotep's Hymn to the Aton or sun-disc, save that references to Yahweh have been tacked on here and there (vv. 1, 24, 31, 33, 34).[31]

These last two examples serve also to remind us that creation stories flourished especially at temples and in cultic celebrations. Examination of the Psalms shows that creation was most frequently spoken of in hymns of praise. Thus the setting in communal life (or "sitz im leben," to use the technical term) for creation references was usually acclamation of God for what he has done as creator. We must especially therefore reckon with the likelihood that when the Yahwist lived, creation hymns and myths were beginning to be more widely heard in Israel and were a growing emphasis at the new temple which Solomon was building in Jerusalem and equipping, often with the help of foreign craftsmen, modeled after what Israel's neighbors knew — creation festivals at a cult center.

Let us now analyze what we have from the Yahwist in Genesis 2. First of all, as the very paragraphing in the RSV makes clear, the unit begins with 2:4*b*, "In the day that Yahweh Elohim made the earth and the heavens. . . ." We have already stressed that, contrary to modern chapter divisions, J's account stretches on through chapter 3, to 4:26. His account of how things got the way they are, thus includes the story of disobedience, of sin, and of expulsion from the garden in these chapters. Von Rad remarks that chapters 2-4 seek to explain "how the chaos of troubled life which surrounds us today developed out of creation"[32] — a chaos which comes not from God the creator, but rather from sinning. He also comments that such an emphasis is "conspicuously isolated in the Old Testament,"[33] and that is glaringly true. What we call "the story of 'the fall'" (Genesis 3) is not really followed up by any Hebrew writer until the Intertestamental Period,[34] and ultimately it is Paul, especially in Romans, who will spell out the meaning of this combination of creation with the fall, the tragedy of a well-created universe and a selfish, egocentric creature named man.

Secondly, we may bracket out 2:10-14, about the four branches of the river in the garden of Eden, as a later intrusion into the story. It is a learned geographical note from ancient times, inserted independently, to underscore the worldwide scope of the tale that is being told.[35]

Thirdly, I would regard details in 2:9 and 3:22, about the "tree of life," as later insertions too. To the main story-line the "tree of knowledge" (2:9, 17; cf. 3:3ff.) is essential; the man and woman eat of it. The tree of life does not, however, play any major role and may be a secondary insertion. At 2:9, moreover, to have two trees "in the *midst* of the garden" is awkward grammatically and logically; 3:3 speaks only of "*the tree* in the middle of the garden" as forbidden. Finally the tree-of-life motif probably reflects a well-known Babylonian story about Adapa or "man," which was inserted here.[36] The detail is not crucial to our analysis, but phrases in 2:9 and 3:22 about the tree of life are probably secondary.[37]

Fourthly, more minute analysis of J in chapter 2, dividing the material into two further sources, J[1] and J[2], as suggested in some commentaries,[38] seems too speculative and unnecessary. We conclude that a single writer, J, has put together a story about the creation of man and woman and how their world got the way it is, marred with a curse upon the ground (3:17ff.) but blessed by a God who is gracious (3:21; cf. 3:15), a narrative that reflects existing traditions and materials, some of them no doubt from Babylon or Canaan. Von Rad wisely says of the story — and it applies to its background too — that it is "part of a traveled road that cannot be traversed again." [39]

With this picture of what the Yahwist wrote, we must now turn to the most important question for us: What, more fully, was his world like when he put together such a narrative, one which is really an affirmation of faith in Yahweh as the creator?

We must remember that always at the heart of Israel's faith was the experience of the exodus, how God delivered his people from Egypt, through the Sea of Reeds, and ultimately led them through the wilderness to the Promised Land. There were also other important traditions, reflecting further experiences with God, for example at Mount Sinai, in the giving of the law, or stories of the patriarchs, Abraham and his descendents. All these elements the Yahwist wove together, building the Sinai traditions into the exodus account, constructing the patriarchal tales into the whole, so that an expanded epic resulted about Yahweh and his deeds. Much of this material had been told and retold over the years around campfires of wanderers and among the clans, and then more recently at the great shrines of the amphictyony or "league of the twelve tribes." The J writer sought to make a unified whole of it.

But as he worked, the world was changing. Israel had shifted from a league of tribes united about a religious center to a nation with a king — first Saul, then David, now his son Solomon. It had become a secular monarchy, like its neighbors, and some old-time die-hards no doubt resented the change; it was to them almost as if Yahweh had been rejected as king (cf. 2 Samuel 8 for a reflection of this attitude).

With a king ruling in Jerusalem came many related changes. In olden times leadership had usually been charismatic, that is, chosen by God to meet an immediate crisis — recall the judges or even the first king, Saul. But now a dynasty, of the house of David, ruled. Previously great store was set in the notion of the "holy war," when God himself would lead his people, suddenly mustered for battle, to victory; now there was a standing army, including mercenaries, even Hittites like Uriah. Once upon a time the *bene Israel* (children of Israel) had been like a congregation or assembly of clans, one close-knit family; now the nation incorporated all peoples who lived within its territorial boundaries, and even Canaanites were included. The one-time Jebusite city of Jerusalem had become the capital, and the rural, nomadic, or agricultural cast to life was being supplemented by a growing commercial class of tradesmen and merchants, with international ties and experiences. A more universal outlook resulted, for Israel's expanding horizons inevitably brought to the people of Yahweh new knowledge of the ways — and gods — of other lands. Solomon himself, through his several marriages with princesses from nearby nations, encouraged this. The average Israelite was coming to know the proverbs, wisdom, stories, and myths of the ancient Near East as never before.

As for religion, the age of Solomon brought changes too. In place of the tent which had long been the center for worship, a magnificent house of God was being built on Mount Zion, a house where cult services appropriate to such a temple and such a nation would be carried out. It continues to be a debated question to what extent the Jerusalem temple developed new year's festivities celebrating creation and annually reviving the fertility of the land by sacred rites, with king and priests reenacting ancient myths through liturgy, as had long been done in Babylonia.[40] It can also be debated exactly what role Zadok the priest played in all this. He was a Jebusite priest retained by David, when Jerusalem fell into his hands, who served to reconcile the Canaanites to the new ruler in Jerusalem, and who as chief priest had opportunity to direct Israel's worship into new paths, closer to Canaanite practice and outlook.[41]

We thus have, at the very time the Yahwist lived and worked, two sometimes related currents set in motion. The one was the temple, with its cult and priests and an interest in creation myths and thought such as Israel had not known before. Out of this developed what we have referred to as "Zion-theology," emphasizing God's choice of Mount Zion for the temple and the house of David for the throne, and stressing creation as a particular theme.[42]

The other current to be seen about 950 B.C. involved what has been called the "Solomonic enlightenment," [43] a new humanism, or even secularization, which resulted from all the changes of old ways and the new international influences on Israel which Solomon brought to his people. Old institutions, in political life, in economics, and in religion, were crumbling. New ones took their place. It was as if windows had been opened and strange breezes were blowing in. Previously unheard of interests proliferated, in the realm of personal experience, psychology, and the inner life. The phrase "the free-thinking era of Solomon" has even been employed, because for some Israelites, no doubt, neither old cult nor the new temple proved satisfying.

In many ways this period of change, as ages of change often are, was a time of crisis. This is particularly true with regard to the "God-question" — where does God speak and act? In the old days of the amphictyony the answer was clear: God works through the cult at the tabernacle, through the priestly ministrations of the

house of Eli; or through seers and charismatics whom God desig-
nates; or through the holy war. His work was to be seen par excel-
lence in the exodus and subsequent wilderness pilgrimage, in his
promise of the land of Canaan as a dwelling place. But now so
much had changed. Memories of the exodus and Sinai no longer
packed the punch they once did. Temple cult was new and different. The holy war was no more, and charismatic moments had been
replaced by the new structure of "Greater Israel."

The question which the Yahwist faced was, "Where is God today?" It would not do merely to repeat ancient shibboleths (even
though he regarded the old stories of the exodus, Sinai, and the
patriarchs as basic). He did not choose to endorse the Zion-theology
of "temple and throne" (though he shared its interest in something
Israelite tradition had not previously said much about: the subject
of creation). It was the other option available to him which the
Yahwist chose: the Solomonic enlightenment — he opted to let God
speak in terms of the secular, profane, and humanistic realm of life.

Gerhard von Rad, in a number of essays,[44] has called attention to
this achievement of the Yahwist who wrote in such a time when the
ancient sacred tradition had come to an impasse. For this theological genius whom we call J took the old traditions of the cult but
retold them with the cultic stripped away, in a "cult-less atmosphere." This is the "Layman's document." He accepted traditions
which Israel seems not to have made much of before, about creation
and how things got the way they are, using stories such as we have
in Genesis 2 and 3 as the vehicle to show man's situation and God's
graciousness. Beyond the old ways in which Yahweh was said to
have spoken in the past, like cult or holy war, he concentrated on
the world of the profane, where God can reveal his workings
equally as well as in the cultic or sacred. He emphasized God's
activity in the quiet, daily events of life and in the recesses of the
human heart. Recall how J shows God at work in the stories of
Jacob or Joseph, not overtly but hiddenly, working even through
sin and disaster. The Yahwist can even see God's hand in political
events.

Thus, to the question "Is God still with Israel; is he at work today?" the Yahwist answered, "Yes, but in different ways than we
have been accustomed to think." Israel has not fallen from God's

hand, for God is now working out his plan through David, in the court, and in the territorial growth of Israel. Indeed, God's providence is at work beyond the land of Israel—he can be with Joseph in an Egyptian jail, in the winning of Rebecca for Jacob at a well in Mesopotamia; even, Ronald Hals has argued, if the story of Ruth is set in this period, in the land of the Moabites.[45] And, we may add, as von Rad does, in the recounting of the story of the man and the woman and the snake in the garden.

One might, judging from the old standpoints, call this new theology of J "secularization" and protest that it involves a different view of revelation. But in a time when faith was challenged to speak about new themes, when it would no longer do just to parrot old promises about "the land," here was how faith spoke about God in a time of change. When Israel might have succumbed to Canaanite religion, the Yahwist took the themes of the world of the day and even its terminology and "Yahweh-ized" them, historicized the myths, de-culticized materials, so that it all became one vast epic of God's saving providence which we treasure to this day.

One specific illustration must suffice. Rites for fertility, for fruitfulness of land and people, were very much a part of religions of the day. Canaanite myths celebrated the annual death and resurrection of Baal. Sacred drama reenacted the marriage of two deities, and temple prostitutes were ready to oblige mere mortals to represent the theme, sacrally symbolizing fertility. It is possible that in Israel, too, a fertility cult grew up, centered in a serpent figure, perhaps even introduced by Zadok the priest.[46] If other nations thus celebrated fecundity in the created realm, why not Israel, identifying Yahweh as its "baal" or master?

The Yahwist did not turn his back on this challenge. But he insisted that it is Yahweh who is lord of fertility, not any serpent or other god. Yahweh in his love, not Baal, is the source of good. He it is who created man, the animals, and vegetation; he it is who sends rain (2:5), who covenants with Adam and promises conquest of the serpent (3:15, 21). Realistically, J insists that sinning does exist, but it is not a cosmic principle inherent in the structure of the world; instead it comes from human disobedience and misbehavior—and if there is punishment, there is forgiveness too. In the garden and beyond, in all the world, Yahweh the creator and Lord, is present, quietly at work.

Thus, for his situation, and from the sources available, the Yahwist has woven a story—if you will, created a myth—for his own purposes, to proclaim a truth. And a magnificent achievement it is! Who, we may ask, has produced such a statement of faith about God and man, creation and life? The author—and one may presume an individual was involved, not a committee or a school—is not identified by name in the Bible. But scholars have proposed two individuals as possibilities. The one is Nathan, the advisor and conscience to David the king (2 Samuel 12). Perhaps he compiled the Yahwist epic as a primer or catechism for Solomon and his sons.[47] The other nominee is even more dramatic: Abiathar, the last surviving priest of the house of Eli, who had served David in his darkest days, but in a dynastic struggle backed the wrong son of David for the throne. Hence, when Solomon became king, he appointed, not Abiathar but, Zadok the Jebusite as priest of his new temple. Abiathar went into exile, at Anathoth, where a later descendent of his named Jeremiah was to prophesy. Here, at Anathoth, in an enforced retirement, Abiathar may have put together the Yahwist epic, as witness of his faith, amid changing times.[48] Whatever the details, whether he be Nathan or Abiathar, the "Yahwist" has shown us how faith spoke about creation in a time of secular crisis.

It is now possible to list some conclusions from this analysis about the Yahwist, which parallel in certain ways those we made concerning 1 Corinthians 8:6.

(1) Here again, just as in our New Testament example, we have language and ideas from the world of the day. Babylonian myth, Canaanite cult and practices, and at times actual words from other cultures (e.g., the term for "mist" or "flood" at 2:6) stand behind and dot the verses of Genesis 2. Here faith speaks in the language of the ancient Near East.

(2) We cannot directly claim that Genesis 2 is a confession of faith (though Genesis 1 is in many ways). But in the Yahwist's account faith is surely at work, speaking. Israel's theology is reworking earlier, and even alien, materials. One can indeed speak of the

Yahwist as "the Bible's First Theologian," as Peter Ellis subtitles his book on him.[49]

(3) Obviously, in this naive but profound narrative, all that is ontological and metaphysical is far removed, but the anthropological and existential elements such as we noted in 1 Corinthians do appear. Man is the starting-point, woman the conclusion of creation; mankind is constantly on center stage. The realm of nature is not featured—save for the serpent. The humanistic side, psychological interest, the sketching of man's situation in life, run deep in the J presentation.

(4) The magnificence of God and his gracious purposes can scarcely be missed here. God acts directly at times, but he also dominates the action when the man and woman are alone or even when the serpent speaks with Eve. God it is who shapes and forms; he it is who can judge, place a curse, and comfort his creatures. The Yahwist writes of God, in his own way, in all he says.

There are dozens of other biblical creation accounts which call for similar treatment such as we have here given 1 Corinthians 8:6 and Genesis 2. Especially relevant are P's version of the beginnings in Genesis 1, and the great "Hymn of Creation and Redemption" in Colossians 1:15-20, for both of which significant studies are available.[50] If the psalms were examined, we would become especially clear on an aspect which we have only in part encountered above: it is what Claus Westermann emphasizes as the doxological aspect of creation hymns, confessions, and narratives. Talk about creation is usually set in the context of praise, glorifying (giving *doxa*) to God.[51]

But we have seen enough to allow us to reach some general conclusions on ways in which faith speaks about creation in the Bible. Our findings may be expressed thus: in the pluralism of scripture's witness, faith—employing materials from the world of the day, reshaping them in light of belief in the God of the exodus who has sent his son Jesus Christ to redeem—faith speaks of the God it knows, as the creator, munificent in his purposes and good, in terms of what his gracious work of creation means for man and his world. Hence the Bible cannot help but sing in praise. Yet at times it cannot ignore, either, the darker side of reality and man's failings.

It remains to be seen what the biblical witness will do with the problem of man, as creation continues.

The "Christ Hymn" of Colossians 1 in Recent Discussion

The hymn about Christ's role in creation and redemption found in the Pauline epistle to Colossae at 1:15-20 has been widely discussed in recent New Testament scholarship and extensively exploited as a foundation stone for thoughts about the "cosmic Christ" and his role in the created universe of nature and men, in ecumenical discussion over the past decade or so. So pivotal has this passage become that some attention to it seems called for here, beyond a mere footnote reference to literature on the topic originally envisioned at the end of this chapter (note 50, above). There is surely a grandeur of vision evoked by this passage. But exegetically how true are some of the ideas "piggy-backed" onto Colossians 1:15-20? Since the verses were above all injected into wider christological consideration at a meeting of the World Council of Churches at New Delhi, India, in 1961, the matter makes for especially interesting treatment against the panorama of religions in India.

The history of the interpretation of 1:15-20, since Schleiermacher in 1832 isolated it as an independent unit, and its relevance to current discussions about Christ and creation, I have briefly outlined elsewhere, in a research report on the passage in connection with dialogue about "Christ and mankind." [52] The general finding there, that all or part of 1:15-20 is an early Christian hymn cited as a basic part of the argument in Colossians, has, if anything, been further amplified and endorsed by subsequent discussions, and we now have available in English a definitive commentary treatment analyzing the original hymn and the application of it in the letter to Colossae.[53]

Fifteen years ago any student of the New Testament dependent primarily on commentaries in English could not be faulted if he failed to see a hymnic composition underlying Colossians 1.[54] Now the arguments for such a source in 1:15-20 have been so widely and persuasively set forth that probably the majority of scholars—certainly the majority of those who have published on the issue—accept the fact that Colossians 1:12-20 contains hymnic materials, in particular a fragment of a hymn about God used as an "introit" or entrance song (vv. 12-14), followed by the Christ hymn in two stanzas (vv. 15-18a; 18b-20). We may arrange the verses thus (employing the language of the RSV):[55]

HYMN TO THE FATHER

With joy [12] give thanks to the Father,
   who has qualified you to share in the inheritance of the saints
      in light.

[13] He has delivered us from the dominion of darkness
   and transferred us to the kingdom of his beloved Son,
      [14] in whom we have redemption,
         the forgiveness of sins.

HYMN TO CHRIST

Stanza I

[15]*He is* the image of the invisible God,
   the first-born of all creation;
      [16] *For in him all* things were created,
         in heaven and on earth,
            visible and invisible,
         whether thrones or dominions
            or principalities or authorities —
      all things were created through him and for him.
[17] *He* is before all things,
   and in him all things hold together.
[18] *He* is the head of the body.

Stanza II

[18b]*He is* the beginning,
   the first-born from the dead,
      that in everything he might be preeminent.
[19] *For in him all* the fulness of God was pleased to dwell,
   [20] and *through him* to reconcile to himself all things,
      making peace *through him,*
         whether on earth or in heaven.

Comparison of the italicized words in stanzas I and II helps bring out the symmetry of a parallelism that is often even closer in the Greek. Christ is first-born (a) before all creation (v. 15) and (b) from the dead (resurrection as redemption, v. 18*b*). "In him" is a key phrase (verses 16 and 19 begin with the same three words in Greek). Two matching phrases about Christ conclude each stanza (17-18*a* and 20).

Exact details about the structure of the hymn will no doubt continue to be debated,[56] as will the question of whether the author of Colossians who employs this hymn is Paul himself or some assistant or later disciple of his.[57] So will the question of the exact nature of the opponents whom the Pauline author opposes, teachers who seek to make the Colossians their prey by clever use of "philosophy and empty deceit" (2:8). That they were Jewish legalists emphasizing laws and rules (2:16, 20), or gnostics of some sort (cf. the use of the Greek word *plēroma*, "fulness," at 2:9, a typically gnostic term), or a syncretistic group, have all been proposed as answers.[58] What seems clear is that Paul combats some views about Christ from a party which accepts the hymnic material in 1:15-20 as authoritative, with the result that Paul can cite these lines as a basis for the argument he will set forth in 1:20ff. and chapter 2. That there is a christological hymn used as source here can be said to be, however, a point of widespread agreement in recent years.[59]

Those who assume a hymn here have further proposed a background out of which it comes. The ideas in these verses reflect both the Hellenistic world (e.g., v. 17, a Stoic reminiscence) and the outlook and the vocabulary of Judaism and the Old Testament (e.g., "image of God" in v. 15, or the idiom in v. 19, "was pleased to . . ."). Hellenistic Judaism had speculations about wisdom and its role in God's creation of the world.[60] Such themes carried over into Christianity and took shape in hymns such as this one employed by Hellenistic Christians of Asia Minor in praise of Christ. These Christians daringly staked out the whole cosmos as sphere of his lordship, amplifying the claim for Christ far more than 1 Corinthians 8:6 had done. Thus, in the stanza on creation, they spoke, in good Greek fashion, of the world as Christ's "body," just as Stoics spoke of the cosmos as "the body of Zeus." [61] It is probably no accident that most of the parallels to materials in other religions found in Colossians 1:15-20 occur within the stanza on creation rather than in stanza II, where the more characteristically biblical ideas concerning redemption occur.

According to recent analyses, there are also in the New Testament a number of other hymns akin to that at Colossians 1:15-20.[62] Philippians 2:6-11, for example, describes how a preexistent Christ was "with God," came to earth, and then was exalted (in v. 8, "even death on a cross" is assumed to be an addition by Paul to relate the hymn more clearly to "Christ crucified"). First Timothy 3:16 is a six-line lyric about Christ's work in the earthly and heavenly realms (again with no apparent reference to the cross). Hebrews 1:2-3 and the poetic portions of John 1:1-18 (likely vv. 1-5, 10-12, 14) deal with Christ and his role in creation. All such hymns seemingly had a common origin in a Hellenistic Christianity with Jewish roots. All of these lyrics set forth a particular view of Christ, as lord of all the cosmos (of "things in heaven, on the earth, and under the earth," as Philippians 2:10 puts it, referring to the common notion of a three-story universe), and an eschatology that never once refers to any second coming of Christ but stresses a present fulfillment and realization now. Enthusiasm about Christ's present lordship marks these hymns, and it is a fair guess to presume they were joyously chanted on cultic occasions, as when converts were initiated into and attached to this Lord Christ by baptism.

To turn to modern discussion for a moment, it is precisely the Christic view of the entire world embodied in such hymns, where the Lord Christ is declared already to rule all things, that has commended Colossians 1:15-20 to those setting forth a "cosmic Christ." For those who wish to emphasize a lord permeating "all things," in nature and total humankind, such verses are the obvious starting point biblically.

Perhaps the first to address himself to such matters in rather recent times, at least in Western theology—in some ways the significant voice — was Allan D. Galloway, whose book *The Cosmic Christ* was published in 1951.[63] Believing the concept of "salvation" to have become "shrunken and dwarfed almost to extinction" in its meaning,[64] he set out to explore the broader aspects of the theme given currency in the phrase "cosmic redemption." How far is salvation operative? How big is the arena of God's saving work? How far does the power of Christ extend? Needless to say, in seeking to explore what he feels is the "development towards a doctrine of cosmic redemption in the Bible" and then in the church fathers, and in discussing how modern views of the universe call for new solutions, Galloway must wrestle with many of the problems which confront us in this study, especially the use of cosmic imagery in apocalyptic passages, plus many more aspects from philosophy (e.g., in the thought of Kant and Hegel) which go untouched in our treatment. Needless to say, Colossians looms largest in his study of the scriptural evidence in moving towards Galloway's conclusions that "the Christ came not only to individuals, but to the whole universe, and that His work is significant for the whole of creation. . . . Expanding horizons made it necessary to expand the scope of the hoped-for redeeming act of God. When once this process had started there was no logical stopping point until the farthest parts of the universe were related in some positive way to the Redeeming Act." [65] Such a scope of grace, with the Colossians passage as "text" and biblical base, was injected into ecumenical discussion by Professor Joseph Sittler's address at the New Delhi assembly of the World Council of Churches in 1961.[66]

But recent exegesis is not finished with the Colossians passage when it has isolated a hymn with its grand vision of lordship in 1:15-20. Modern biblical scholarship is also at pains to tell us how the author of Colossians used this hymn and with what intent.[67] We must ask not only after the tradition which Paul (or the Pauline author of Colossians) has taken over but also about the "redaction," i.e., the way he has edited it and interpreted the hymn by means of his own comments which follow (1:21ff.). Presumably here the apostolic voice is most surely heard when he comments on what he quotes.

It is clear that into the Hellenistic Christian hymn has been inserted, first, an identifying phrase at the end of stanza I, to make clear how the phrase "his body" is to be understood by Christians. According to Colossians 1:18a it is not "the world" (as in Stoicism) that is Christ's body, but rather Christ

is the head of his body, *the church.*

Of course, it is structurally illogical to have a reference to the church in the stanza on creation; the church is a community of redemption, into which believers have been delivered by the action of the Son (1:13f.). But so intent is the writer to make the point, regular in Pauline thought, of the church as the body of Christ (cf. 1 Cor. 12:27; Rom. 12:5, etc.), that he destroys some of the symmetry of the hymn in order to prevent any notion that Christ is embodied in the cosmos. Better bad poetry than misleading theology! He reiterates the point at 1:24 (". . . for the sake of his body, that is, the church").

Secondly, our author-editor added a phrase in v. 20 to explain *how* God "reconciled all things" and "made peace" through Christ. It was "by means of the blood of his cross" (v. 20c). The term in the hymn "fulness of God" (v. 19, literally "all the *plēroma*") was susceptible of various interpretations in the world of the day, including a reference to the upper part of the spirit world between God and man (later gnostics especially were to use it thus; the modifying term, "of God," is an insertion in English translations not found in the Greek). Myths of the period depicted cosmic peace as being established in a variety of ways by redeemer figures. The Pauline author of Colossians wants to make sure, by his insertion, that redemption is tied securely to the death of Jesus on the cross, a point he reiterates at 1:21 ("you . . . he has now reconciled in his body of flesh by his death").

Besides these two inserts into the hymn itself, the author of Colossians also provides a corrective by comments in the verses that follow. His method of interpreting comes out if we pay attention to what he stresses and what he ignores of the content of the hymn. So it is that he does *not* pick up the theme of creation (stanza I) but only redemption (stanza II). And he does this in terms of people ("you . . ."), not of the cosmos (1:21ff.). Moreover, when he does allude to the cosmic powers listed in the hymn (1:16), he does not suggest that these will be reconciled under the category of "all things" (1:20) but rather he holds them to have been disarmed and led captive in the triumph of Christ (2:15). Above all, there is no hint that Christ's existing lordship suffices or that everything is already as Christic as it needs to be. Rather the advance of Christ into the world of men's hearts must come through the toil of missionaries like Paul (1:29), through the proclamation of the word (1:28), in the work of the church as "missionary body of Christ." [68]

It would, of course, be untrue to pretend that all exegetes agree on every detail as we have outlined our analysis of tradition and redaction above. Even in a discussion among Catholic and Protestant experts who united in the basic assumption that there is an earlier hymn used and interpreted by the Pauline author, there did appear a difference of opinion over whether one should stress the *contrast* between the hymnic source and its apostolic application or the *unity* between source and apostle.[69] What is agreed, however, rather widely is that Colossians contains a hymn, with its own theology, and the epistle has developed the ideas of the hymn in a particular way. We thus have two theologies before us, however much we may wish to harmonize or contrast them: that of the hymn, with its cosmic Christ of creation and redemption; and that of the finished epistle, with its corrective clauses and missionary thrust.

The thought of the hymn, by itself, we have seen, has genuine appeal to some today. Professor Sittler's evocative usage, with his "Christology of nature," and Galloway's affirmation of a "cosmic Christ" have appealed to many in the Eastern Orthodox tradition and in Roman Catholic theology (where grace in Christ is held to "perfect nature"). Sittler's address also signaled a new direction in the program of ecumenical discussion within the Faith and Order Movement, which had for many years been dealing with classical problems of Christology (and had often reached an impasse) and then had broadened in the 1950s to take up "Christ and the Church" (and again had come to impasses). The program now became "Christ, World, Church," in that order, as if Christ were present in the world as much as (or even more than) he works in his church. According to the hymn (1:18a), he does permeate the world, as "head of the body," the world he created (though according to the letter as a whole, he seeks to penetrate the world of men through the church, his body, and its apostolic mission). From "Christ in the world" it is but a step to claim that, in one way or another, all men must somehow be "in Christ" the creator and redeemer, and that therefore they are, even if they know it not, "anonymously Christian."

Such thinking has particular appeal in a land like India where there are many religions (though Hinduism is predominant) and Christians are a tiny minority (two and a half percent in all of India). The desire of those attracted to Christ in such a scene often is fervently to assert his lordship over all and to suggest he somehow permeates into even those other religions which do not openly acknowledge him. But while "cosmic Christology" has attracted considerable worldwide attention in the past decade, in Europe and America and ecumenical discussion generally,[70] two surprises await the investigator who tries to trace out this theme in discussion in India. The first is the relative dearth of articles, let alone books, on the subject since 1961 in Indian publications; the second is the discovery that "cosmic Christology" and its attendant claims about Christ permeating all men is actually "old stuff" in Indian theology. In fact, one reason why so little has been done with the New Delhi theme in India may be that much of it, in one way or another, has been said before!

The first point, consideration of "cosmic Christology" in India since 1961: there has been remarkably little published on the theme, either in English-language journals or, so far as I can ascertain, in any of the native-language publications (Hindi, Tamil, Telugu, Malayalam, etc.), whether by Westerners in India or indigenous theologians.[71] Perhaps this is because classical problems like the Trinity or the humanity of Christ still occupy great attention. Perhaps it is that engagement with the other great world religions has not taken up this specific avenue of rapproachment. At any rate, treatments and references are comparably rare to the New Delhi theme, in proportion to what one would expect.

The most significant discussion on the "cosmic Christ" in the Indian scene has probably been that which took place at a Protestant-Roman Catholic Colloquium at Serampore in 1965, papers from which were published in two issues of the *Indian Journal of Theology* the next year.[72] While presentations were included on the patristic evidence, recent interpretations, the relationship to other religions, and to the "Asian Revolution," and the "Colossian Vision in Theology and Philosophy," I find the most pertinent treatment for our concerns that by J. C. Hindley, of Serampore College, on "The Christ of Creation in New Testament Theology." It is valuable especially because Hindley comes at the overall problem from a viewpoint which does *not* go along with the theory of a pre-Pauline hymn behind Colossians 1:15-20, and does recognize that the term *panta,* "all things," in these verses is precisely the basis for speaking of "Christ in Hinduism" (as does Raymond Panikkar; see below) or "Christ in the Asian Revolution" (emphasized by writers connected with the Christian Institute for the Study of Religion and Society, Bangalore). Yet Hindley is in basic agreement with our general positions, for, he cautions, the pertinent references in Colossians 1 to the cosmos are connected with Christ's work in *creation,* not in the *new* creation. "The first chapter of Colossians is built on the contrast between the old and the new creation: in both cases Christ is *prototokos* ["first-born"], but they are two and not one—a vital point which was overlooked, I think, by the otherwise noteworthy paper published by J. Sittler on this theme at the New Delhi Assembly. . . ." [73] Hindley also notes the tendency to overlook creation as "fallen," and stresses, as we have, that affirmations about creation arise only out of the experience of salvation. This, he adds, is to desert "cosmology in favor of soteriology," but he pleads guilty to the charge, for salvation is precisely what he finds central.

Our second point: that, upon investigation, one finds that the "cosmic Christ" emphasis and even some of the terms lately used have appeared before in Indian theology, indeed in the nineteenth century. There has, of course, long been a quest on the part of Indian Christianity to relate faith in Christ to its situation in the vast subcontinent, to a thought-pattern and culture that is non-Western but rich and diversified. Christianity, lest it appear as a "Western import," must come to terms with the Hindu ethos and express itself in Eastern, Asian ways. Thus, as early in 1858 Indian Christians attempted to form "The Hindu Church of Jesus Christ" and in 1887 "The Calcutta Christo Samaj (Society)." Again and again the assertions have been heard, "Christ is Asiatic"; the Christian mysteries can be found, at least foreshadowed, in the *Vedas* (Hindu scriptures); "we are Hindu Christian, as thoroughly Hindu as Christian"; and even, "Are not Hindus Christians?" (in that, beneath Hinduism, one can find the "true religion" from the "days of creation," which conforms with "Christianity as old as creation").[74]

Specifically, the first nudge in this direction came, not from Christian converts, but from Hindus attracted to the figure of Jesus who never quite made the step of formal profession and membership in the church. Thus Keshab Chandra Sen (1838-1884), who organized the Brahma Samaj along the lines of a Christian church, and later established a "Church of the New Dispensation" complete with sacraments (including a communion of rice and water), stressed a logos-Christ, the "Journeying God" who since creation is bringing "divine humanity" to all men in what, to employ Teilhard de Chardin's phrase, amounts to their "Christification"—in Sen's phrase, "to make every man Christ." [75] Sen thus set forth a "hidden Christ," who "is in you even when you are unconscious of his presence," suggesting an evolutionary process which "links the incarnation with the whole creative process." [76] The result would be a "Christo-centric harmony of religions in general and of Hinduism and Christianity in particular." [77]

This sort of view of Christ was injected into Christian circles, specifically Roman Catholic ones, by Bhavani Charan Banerji (1861-1907), a Brahman from Bengal who in 1891 was baptized into the Anglican Church but almost immediately joined the Roman Catholic Church, rightly sensing, perhaps, that its principle "Grace does not obliterate but perfects the natural" (*Gratia non tollit naturam sed perficit*) gave greater possibility for the rapproachment with Hinduism which he sought.[78] Choosing the name "Theophilus" ("friend or lover of God"), which could be rendered as "friend of Brahman," he thereafter worked in saffron robe as a Catholic *sannyasi* (mendicant, reflecting the fourth and final stage of Brahman life), a would-be reformer in Catholicism (for which, his publications ended on the Index of forbidden reading) and an ardent Indian nationalist (for which he was charged by the British with revolution). He held himself to be a "Hindu Catholic," born Hindu, reborn Catholic, combining both henceforth. In particular he sought to find in the *Vedas* an Indian replacement for the Hebrew Old Testament as "preparation for Christ" (hence he has sometimes been dubbed the "Indian Clement of Alexandria," [79] after the great church father who saw in Greek philosophy a path to Christ alongside the Old Testament). Brahmabandhab Upadyav ("Friend of God, teacher"), as he became known, found the Trinity in Sanskrit hymns and Christ the logos already present in Indian Vedanta thought. His hope was for a synthesis combining Hinduism's highest with the theology of Thomas Aquinas: upon the natural truths of Hindu thought should be built the supernatural religion of Christ.[80]

Many of the same ideas, plus an emphasis on "new creation," appear in the more recent writings of a layman, lawyer, and judge, Pandipeddi Chenchiah (1886-1959), a convert from Hinduism.[81] Here again we find the suggestion of a relationship between Hinduism and Christianity and the argument that Hindu literature is more relevant in India than the Old Testament as a preparation for the New. Here, too, Christ (but not the church) is central, what Chenchiah called "the raw fact of Christ," the man who is "a new creation—the Lord and Master of a new creature branch of Cosmos," the one in whom "creation mounts a step higher," "the origin of the species of the Sons of God." [82] Writing against the kind of Barthian theology exemplified in the world of missions by Hendrik Kraemer's *The Christian Message in a Non-Christian World* (1938), Chenchiah stressed "lifefulness," not sin, and saw Jesus as "the head of a new world order," inaugurating that new creation where the children of God evolve and the kingdom comes, by "the *yoga* [union, or way of achieving union] of the Spirit." Romans 8:19, about creation waiting for "manifestation of the sons of God," points to a "process of 'reproducing the image of Christ' or even of 'becoming Christ.'" Small wonder that Boyd calls his "the theology of the new creation." [83] Chenchiah is quite clear that it is Christianity which is the new Man, Christ is the first fruits and the *adi-purusha* [original Man] of a new creation; but Hinduism represents "the final fruits of the old." [84]

To bring this brief survey closer to the present, we note two further names among theologians in India, Paul David Devanandan (1901-1962), professor at United Theological College, Bangalore, and subsequently Director of the Christian Institute for the Study of Religion and Society there; and Father Raymond Panikkar, born in Spain in 1918 of a Hindu father and a Spanish Roman Catholic mother, now teaching at Varanasi (Benares) and Harvard. Devanandan was, just prior to his death, one of the major speakers at the World Council's New Delhi meeting. Like Chenchiah, he at

times reacted against Barth and found a major theme in "new creation." He saw this concept as involving the purpose of God for the
whole creation. But new creation must come, he argued, not by
evolution, but conversion (a word often unpopular in India, which,
however, he resolutely defended). Devanandan's agenda also called
for reshaping Hinduism's view of creation, so as to stress God's
continuous activity and his concern for all redemptively.[85] Panikkar
has become known especially for his book, *The Unknown Christ of
Hinduism* (1964),[86] which holds Christ is hiddenly present in Hinduism to make it an effective means of salvation; but this Christ
in Hinduism is still veiled and "has to grow up" and "be recognized" and "be crucified there," before there can be a "risen Hinduism"—which will be Christianity.

Enough has been said of these specific examples that we can
see how through a number of Indian thinkers runs the idea of a
Christ working throughout creation, in all of human history, specifically and especially in the Hindu world, bringing about a new
creation for the cosmos. If interest in this "cosmic Christ" of creation has not been multiplied in that land since Sittler's New Delhi
address, it is in part because these concerns have for a century
been characteristic of some theologians at least in the Indian scene.
Repeatedly in India there has been expressed the notion of Christ's
cosmic lordship, permeating even Hinduism, and the hope of a
new creation. More recently, in world ecumenical circles, we see
the notion of all men being somehow "in Christ" (even though
they may be individually unaware of it); the emphasis on "world"
as arena of grace and a concern for the environment have opened
new vistas for his lordship.

More often than not, Colossians, especially 1:15-20, has been
cited as the biblical basis for such thinking. In terms of recent
exegesis we have found that the underlying hymn does talk of
Christ as Lord and creator of "all things," and suggests the world
to be his body, so that, seemingly, all men are his and so is the
world of nature. But the Pauline author of the finished epistle dis-
plays little interest in such points, even though he quotes the entire
hymn. Instead, he emphasizes church, mission, preaching, witness—
that is the way to make real Christ's lordship corporately in the
wider world.

The hymn thus offers a toe-hold for cosmic-Christ speculations but the total intent of the Book of Colossians here points in a different direction. While it remains for us, in Chapter IV, to ask what the Bible means by "new creation," the final impression from Colossians 1-2 as a whole is against what Bishop Lohse, in his commentary, terms "a newly advocated 'ecumenical' theology": the emphasis at 1:20 on Christ's atoning death, i.e., the Pauline "theology of the cross," he says, "arrests all attempts to utilize the hymn for the purposes of a natural or cosmic theology." [87]

A decade after New Delhi, Professor Sittler has had occasion to reexamine "The Scope of Christological Reflection" [88] as he had proposed it cosmically then. His attempt in 1961 at intersecting "New Testament images with modern man's engagement and transactions with the modern world" he holds to have been apposite and to be confirmed by subsequent events, so that only "the whole creation" will do as the "necessary scope of christological speech." He is aware, however, of the trends in exegesis that question some of the conclusions drawn from the "Christ hymn." In reply he states, "For a long time the extraordinary amplitude of Colossians 1:15-22 [20?] was reduced to dogmatically less embarrassing size by dismissing it as superheated rhetoric fashioned by the writer to relate Christian claims for Christ to the scope of Gnostic speculation, and indeed, possibly to have borrowed its images from that tradition. This tactic is no longer possible." [89]

Why, precisely, it is no longer possible to question the rhetoric and ask about gnosticizing overtones, we are not told. Nor is there any discussion of the text. Rather, an unpublished paper by a colleague at Chicago, Paul Ricoeur, is invoked, which distinguishes between "ostensive" and the "nonostensive references" in a text. The former have to do with the plain and apparent sense, intended by the author; the latter, with a sense that involves, not what the author meant or his situation implied, but what the reader today perceives it to mean for himself. The "nonostensive" thus becomes not the meaning *in* a text but that "*in front of* it," what is termed the ". . . modes of being in the world which the text opens up and discovers for me." [90] On this basis Colossians is declared valid in a quest for a Christology to serve the environmental crisis and for appropriate belief statements for today.

One fears, however, that such an approach can make of the Scriptures—and all written documents, including what modern theologians write—a subjective hunting ground which can be taken to mean whatever any reader wants it to mean today or in the future. The result would be a breakdown of rational inquiry—why bother with exegesis at all, if the nonostensive meaning can ride roughshod over what the meaning of the speaker or author is established to be? Then scripture would really have what Luther, in his dispute with the medieval Schoolmen, called a "wax nose," one that can be twisted and moulded by everyone, to give the profile desired. Noble as a "cosmic Christology" may be and relevant to current needs, we must ask if it comes anywhere near to what the biblical author intended—or is it closer to the hymnic rhetoric he so carefully seeks to curb?

I have no doubt that there was a type of early Christianity which enthusiastically projected Christ's lordship over "all." The danger was that such a Christology would forget the costly cross of Jesus of Nazareth, if not the man Jesus himself, for a vaguer "Christ figure," and the servant-witness role of the church would be forgotten in favor of grander pretensions of glory. The hymns of this type of Christianity well fit certain moods today, but we must be alert to the dangers introduced thereby.

During my brief stay in India I sensed a great concern on the part of some Christians to relate their faith to the surrounding culture (just as Americans, Germans, Englishmen and others have been alert to do). Once I attended an experimental worship service planned by such Christians to celebrate the Hindu festival of Dasara. Dasara is a joyous season marking Rama's victory over the evil Ravana, king of Ceylon. As part of the service, scenes were acted out and selections read dealing with Rama's victory, which comes through his obedience, and with the faithfulness of his brother Lakshman and the suffering of his wife Sita, in the epic *Ramayana*. The scripture reading from the New Testament was Philippians 2:6-11, now widely identified as a hymn, from the type of Christianity which gave us Colossians 1:15-20,[91] about Christ's victory through obedience and his ensuing exaltation.

The implications seemed all too clear. Christ in the hymn, and Rama in the epic, represent god figures in the history of religions who teach a similar lesson. The danger — a constant threat through Hinduism, well exemplified in the way it has absorbed other religions, e.g., Buddhism which has virtually disappeared from the land of its origins — is that Christ will be seen as just another *avatar* or incarnation of the divine hero; Christianity will be absorbed into the amazingly broad and tolerant synthesis of the Hindu mind. Unless — and this was precisely the danger St. Paul saw and why he added a specific reference to the cross of Jesus at Philippians 2:8 — unless it be remembered that the Christ is Jesus, a concrete Jewish man, who was crucified in A.D. 30. That is the question mark put behind all "cosmic figures" in Hellenistic hymns and modern theology: Is it of Jesus that we speak, are the features of the Crucified One clearly discernible?

Faith, at moments of ecstasy, tends to talk extravagantly. We need its horizon-bursting optimism. But we require also honest realism, and roots ever firm in the matrix of redemption in Christ. How faith speaks in bright moments is an acid test, just as is how it speaks in dark days. As creation continued, we must ask, how else did biblical faith talk of God, redemption, and the created world?

III

Creation Continues—
Redemptively

Over the centuries after the Yahwist, the earliest theologian in the Bible, had told his tale of God and mankind at the beginning and beyond, the story of creation continued to be recounted in Israel from the standpoint of faith. The Priestly writer's version, written after the exile, around 450 B.C., though it is based on much earlier traditions, is of course well-known, preserved for us in Genesis 1; its very location at the forefront of the canon gives it a special prominence. The so-called Elohist source (E), insofar as it has been reconstructed and is extant, contains no creation account.[1] However, Israel's prophets sometimes allude to creation, and the liturgical compositions of her priests and psalmists reflect the theme far more.[2]

All during these centuries, of course, Israel's neighbors to the east, in Mesopotamia, kept on retelling their ancient myths about a cosmic struggle which produced the world. Egypt repeated her many legends. And by the time Hezekiah was on the throne at Jerusalem and the Northern Kingdom had fallen, epics in Greek began to appear about the beginnings of the world. Hesiod's poems, often reflecting Near Eastern myth, were circulating about 700 B.C., and in another hundred years, by the time Jerusalem fell to the Babylonians, Greek thinkers in Asia Minor — the "Milesian School" (again heavily indebted to the East) — had begun to enunciate elements of "Western philosophy," including among other things, discussion of creation.[3] In such ways stories simple and profound about "the beginning" were told.

But creation existed as a living theme in another way, too, during the centuries after the Yahwist, down to the period of the New Testament when Paul was quoting Christian statements on God's creative work (1 Cor. 8:6). As we have understood creation,[4] the concept has to do not merely with beginnings or origins, but also with the dependence of man and his world, of all things living and inanimate, on God. Because this aspect goes on as long as man and life and world endure, creation obviously continues.

We have seen how this aspect of continuing creation is reflected in the formula at 1 Corinthians 8:6 — "we live," and presumably "all things are," in the words of that credo, "for God"; further, it is claimed, we believers and the whole creation exist and live "through Jesus Christ." Another early Christian formulation was to say this even more distinctly when it confessed of the Son not only that "he created the world" but also that "he upholds the universe by his word of power" (Hebrews 1:2-3). In Genesis 2 and 3 this ongoing aspect of creation is reflected in the fact that the Yahwist was anxious not merely to explain how human life began but to account for the nature of life as it is, in a world where hard toil is required to grow a crop, and pregnancy brings pain, where snakes crawl on their belly and are reputed to eat dust — and where God has not forsaken his children, even "east of Eden."

There are implications to be drawn from this persistent biblical concern which does *not* leave God back at the beginning or regard him as the "Great Clock-maker, who wound up the universe and left it to run down," as Deism thought of him. One implication is that God's power and graciousness, shown in making a good world, continue to be felt and make themselves known in constant, daily, even moment-to-moment sustenance. A Latin way of saying this is *creatio continua,* "continuing creation." Jesus put it thus: "Your Father who is in heaven . . . makes his sun rise on the evil and on the good, and sends rain on the just and on the unjust" (Matt. 5:45). The Yahwist said: "While the earth remains, seedtime and harvest, cold and heat, summer and winter, day and night [all of these, in the opinion of the J writer responsible for Genesis 8:22, being God's good gifts in creation] shall not cease." In nature the Creator's mercies continue. The classical theological term for all this is, of course, the providence of God.

But such a notion of continuing creation also implies that God's great mercy, seen in his constant care, and his love, shown in the initial creation, which faith confesses, will from time to time break forth anew, quite apart from the constancy of nature, in history. Mercy and love will manifest themselves redemptively. Thus, when Israel gets into dire straits, God in his loving care will send prophets or warriors or poets or pastors, or later on a good shepherd and anointed One, as well as new prophets and apostles to lead and re-create his people. Will not continuing creation, if it involves God, take the shape at times of saving acts and redemption?

All this, of course, is to raise afresh the question of the much debated relationship of creation and redemption. In presenting examples from 1 Corinthians and Genesis, we have assumed that the person or persons speaking were members of a redeemed community, the people of God taking shape in the old or new Israel. In those instances cited, that is obviously so. It is "for us" who confess Jesus as Christ and Lord that he is mediator of creation and preserver of the universe (1 Cor. 8:6). And such a confession presumes faith in Jesus as savior. In the case of the Yahwist it is his faith, in the God who had constituted Israel a people by his deliverance from Egypt, that allows him to say God manifests a graciousness which continues throughout history and can be traced back to the very beginning of time.

But may there not have been some Israelites (or early Christians) who put a primacy on creation rather than upon redemptive events? Were there not times when faith spoke of creation by itself, without any reference to redemption? Might there not have been occasions when the memory of the exodus faded, or the significance of the cross grew obscure, but the created world and the regularity of seedtime and harvest loomed large? (Centuries later, we may remind ourselves, it was not the passover events, old or new, the release from Egyptian bondage or Jesus' resurrection which filled the heart of Immanuel Kant, the philosopher-theologian of Königs-berg in the late eighteenth century, with awe, but "the starry sky above.") We have already seen how various traditions circulated separately in ancient Israel — the Sinai tradition, the stories of the patriarchs, the account of the occupation of the land of Canaan. At the least, it must be admitted, creation materials, too, could have

circulated alone. Such surely was the case with a Babylonian creation epic like *Enuma elish*. The question is, To what extent did this
happen in the biblical community?

The differing situations of ancient Israel and primitive Christianity may well be distinguished here. For the early church we have
already seen that a credo like 1 Corinthians 8:6 could circulate
by itself without any reference to redemptive events — save for the
important qualification that the community which in this formula
confessed Christ as Lord and agent of creation regarded itself as
separated from the bulk of the world ("to us," who through Christ
live). It is a far cry from this — and impossible, in my mind — to
demonstrate that there was ever any sort of early Christianity, ever,
which made statements about Christ and creation without having
some sort of significant christological confession about Jesus as a
redeemer. A crucified criminal can scarcely be proclaimed to have a
connection with the creation of the world without assuming he is
Lord, or a despised Jewish Galilean be proclaimed as mediator of
life without the experience that through him God has provided
new life; and that regularly involved confession of his death and
resurrection as salvific in some way. In cases in our New Testament
texts where there is talk of Christ and creation, there is also usually
direct reference to the salvation-event. For example, Colossians
1:15-20 speaks both of Christ through whom "all things were created" (1:16) and of "the blood of his cross" which brings reconciliation (1:20). The Prologue to the Gospel of John, no matter
in what way we analyze that hymnic passage (1:1ff.), seems not
only to say "all things were made through the Word" (1:3) but
also to speak of his redemptive entry into the world (1:10-12).[5]
In short, I find it hard to locate evidence for any kind of early
Christianity which had a "christological cosmogony" (or account
giving Jesus Christ a place in the making of the world) without
also a soteriological Christology (a statement which speaks of him
as savior).

With Old Testament Israel the matter is more complex. Here
God, not Christ, is involved, and over the centuries it became
common to speak of God in so many ways that talk of him as
creator and sustainer, without reference to his redemptive deeds,
certainly seems possible. Moreover, the very fact that Israel's neigh-

bors talked of their gods in creation terms and nature categories would encourage Israelites to speak of Yahweh likewise, omitting reference to his redemptive work in history. The likelihood of a "creation faith" in Israel, existing separately from "redemption faith" — this appears prima facie evident, and has indeed been claimed.[6] By a few, Yahweh has even been said to have been a creator deity, but that depends on some very uncertain assumptions, including the presumption that the etymology of YHWH had something to do with the causative sense of the verb "to be" and meant "I 'cause to be' what comes into existence."[7]

Whatever the details, we must in effect admit that at times the concept of God in ancient Israel could become "creation-centered," for in some situations creation was a — or the — crucial front. We must certainly grant, too, that some Israelites no doubt saw God in Baal-like terms, as a nature deity wearing only dimly the features of the god of history stressed in the exodus traditions. But to what extent did "creation faith" become a separate category, and creation a (or the) major emphasis?

Answering this problem has led to vigorous debate. Sometimes it takes the form of discussion about whether Israel had a creation epic, like *Enuma elish*, where Yahweh did battle with a chaos monster, out of which conflict creation of the world ensued.[8] Another form of the discussion is whether at the Jerusalem temple there was an annual New Year's celebration like that in Babylon, with myth and ritual, celebrating creation and the renewal of fertility in the land.[9] At times this discussion takes the shape of exegetical battles over interpretation of a specific verse in a prophet, or how far an allusion in a psalm can be pressed.[10]

Chiefly, however, consideration of this question has centered on the place the doctrine of creation had in Israelite theology. Was it minor and on the margin, viewed in light of redemptive history — to use a formula where R denotes "redemption" and C equals "creation," did redemption take priority over creation, $\frac{R}{C}$? Or was it major and even at times central, so that creation dominated references to redemption, $\frac{C}{R}$?

The most widely accepted judgment is probably the opinion of Gerhard von Rad, offered in 1936, that "in genuinely Yahwistic belief the doctrine of creation never attained to the stature of a relevant, independent doctrine"; rather it was "invariably related, and indeed subordinated, to soteriological considerations." [11] In other words: $\frac{R}{C}$ ——. A good number of subsequent investigators have endorsed or borne out that opinion.[12] The difficulty with von Rad's answer, in addition to qualifications that subsequent studies by him or others may have introduced, lies in the phrase "genuinely Yahwistic belief." Proponents of greater emphasis on creation fear that this phrase allows any passage maximalizing the creation motif to be shunted aside as not "genuinely Yahwistic," whatever that means.

The alternative's to von Rad's view can be classified in two categories. (1) Those who make of creation and nature a distinct and major theme, important in Israel, at times central. Sometimes this emphasis even minimalizes the role of God in history and redemptive events, and makes Israel like its ancient Near Eastern neighbors. This alternative is usually expressed in connection with treatment of an individual biblical author or treatment of a particular verse.[13] (2) There is also the attempt to make creation a major category in Israelite thought but to view it within the framework of salvation history. This position, often from the school of heilsgeschichte, emphasizes creation more than von Rad does but does not turn it in opposition to redemptive acts in history. Such a position has been worked out in detail by the Swedish scholar Gösta Lindeskog.[14]

With regard to this disputed question on the relation of creation and redemption in the Old Testament — which has been posed above both in terms of how continuing creation may have manifested itself salvifically and of whether creation was a basic category in its own right or is to be seen regularly in relation to redemption — we shall proceed by examining three types of illustrative passages. First a few examples from Israel's prophets before the exile and second some psalms will be taken up. Then third, as major evidence, the extensive material in Deutero-Isaiah will be discussed. Appended to our discussion of Isaiah 40-55 must be some reference to Isaiah 56-66, where the phrase "new heavens and new earth" occurs, as link to later developments.

A. Creation Imagery in the Preexilic Prophets

The most surprising fact about the prophets is the paucity of references to creation which can be traced back genuinely to their preaching or oracles before the Babylonian exile. The number of such examples in the prophetic corpus is not overly large to begin with, perhaps two dozen or so in the original Isaiah (742-687 B.C.), Jeremiah (627-580), and the minor prophets Hosea and Amos (eighth century), Nahum and Habakkuk (seventh century), and including Zechariah and Malachi (sixth century and later) and even Ezekiel (postexilic).[15] (Isaiah 40-66 will be treated below, in sections C and D.) Of these two dozen examples a number have been termed later interpolations by many commentators.

Taking the situation as a whole, we have good reason to conclude that the prophets before 586 B.C. did not refer to creation overly much and that, during the exile period in Babylon, creation became a much more prominent category. For Second Isaiah alone, writing during the Babylonian captivity, will provide a dozen pertinent passages from the period around 540 B.C. This proliferation of interest in creation during and after the exile, accounts for, incidentally, the later insertion of references to creation in the books of the preexilic prophets as they have been transmitted to us; their editors during and after the exile wanted to bring this theme to the fore in the final versions of the prophets' oracles which they were compiling.

We need not suppose, however, that Israel never heard or spoke of creation in the period between the Yahwist and the exile, even if the prophets do not refer much to it. There was in use, of course, the Yahwist's epic which began with creation. Although the E writer and perhaps the Northern Kingdom generally, where the Elohist was active, shunned a creation account, the traditions later written down by the Priestly writer were probably also available in oral form, throughout these centuries. Some think there was even an Israelite epic about Yahweh fighting against the chaos monster, similar to what the Babylonians and Canaanites recited of their gods. Above all, in temple circles and the psalms creation was celebrated; of that we shall speak in a moment.

Given so many uncertainties, however, the general situation in the eighth and seventh centuries, when the prophets were active, may be sketched in at least four ways. One is to assume that, while creation myths and legends abounded in the ancient Near Eastern world, and the prophets reflect these at times, approving or disapproving aspects of them, no such myth existed in Israel; and that these foreign myths were only later taken up by the Priestly writer and then purified for Israelite use.

A second model is to assume that the ancient Near Eastern myths and legends were not only known to the prophets but actually embodied in an Israelite version of this myth; that such an Israelite creation-battle epic was used at least in Judah and was transmitted orally until the time the Priestly writer took up this Israelite myth and recast it in accord with his own theology.

A third way of looking at the situation is to suppose that there was an Israelite myth about the creation-battle, and that there was general sympathy toward it on the part of the prophets; hence they allude to it but never really quote it much. In this view, the version we have by the Priestly writer in Genesis 1 would be a later reworking, influenced by Israel's oral creation myth and the prophets' references.

The fourth possibility holds that what we know in Genesis 1 was really composed rather early, before the exile, though it may have been reworked by the Priestly writer in the fifth century B.C. Since the Genesis 1 version does not include any reference to a battle between Yahweh and the forces of chaos — the only vestige of this is the word translated "the deep" in 1:2, in Hebrew *thehom,* which etymologically is an equivalent of "Tiamat," the chaos dragon in Babylonia — this fourth view posits an Israelite creation-battle myth circulating alongside of an early version of Genesis 1 before the exile. In this case the prophets could have been influenced by both an Israelite myth of the battle between God and Tiamat and a version of Genesis 1.

It will be seen that in three of these four theories the likelihood of a myth in Israel about a battle between Yahweh and a fierce monster, out of which creation resulted, is assumed. I regard such an Israelite myth as a distinct possibility, though we do not have the text of it and the fragmentary Canaanite parallels we know to date leave a lot to be explained.[16] A few reflections of this myth in the prophets will show how precarious the evidence is, yet also why a goodly number of scholars have conjectured that Jerusalem and Judah knew such a myth.

We begin with a brief reference at Jeremiah 4:23. Here the prophet, in a vision of the earth laid waste by God's judgment, depicts the mountains as quaking, the birds as gone, the land a desert, and the cities in ruins (4:23-26). It is as if an H-bomb had devastated things, in the "fierce wrath" of God. The opening phrase which Jeremiah employs is this:

I looked on the earth, and lo, it was *waste and void;*
and to the heavens, and they had no light.

That reminds us of the situation at the beginning of Genesis 1: light has not been created yet (1:3), and the earth was "without form and void" (1:2). But the parallel is even more precise. The Hebrew phrase at Jeremiah 4:23 is an assonant one, *"thohu wabohu,"* and exactly the same phrase turns up at Genesis 1:2. Did Genesis 1 get this phrase from the prophet Jeremiah, as model one suggests, or did Genesis 1 in an early form provide it for Jeremiah's use (theory four), or did perhaps both prophet and Priestly writer derive it from a common source, some ancient Near Eastern myth (models two or three)? The whole exercise is exasperating, a bit like the question which came first, the chicken or the egg, but the problem arises elsewhere too. For example, compare Jeremiah 31:35-37, about "the sun for light by day" and "the moon and the stars for light by night," and Jeremiah 10:2 ("the signs of the heavens") with Genesis 1:14-18.

A longer example comes in the Book of Amos, where three doxologies about creation occur at Amos 4:13, 5:8-9, and 9:5-6. Magnificent in imagery they are. Anyone who studied Old Testament under one of my seminary professors, Dr. Charles M. Cooper, will recall these verses vividly, for Professor Cooper made students construct out of Old Testament phrases a "credo" parallel to the faith of the Apostles' Creed. These verses in Amos provided for

Article I of such a creed the most striking summaries on creation in the entire Hebrew scriptures.

However, virtually every commentary agrees these doxologies are intrusive where they stand in the present Book of Amos. 9:5-6, for example, clearly interrupts, with its creation language, the flow of thought in 9:1-4 and 9:7ff. In the verses that precede and follow, Yahweh is speaking in the fifth vision which Amos reports, and he is speaking in judgment on his people. 9:5-6 intrudes with a third-person reference to God as creator.

The most attractive solution to the problem of these doxological fragments about creation in Amos is that proposed by Hans Walter Wolff in his recent commentary.[17] He assumes that all three passages can be fitted together, in a hymn of three strophes, each ending with the phrase "Yahweh is his name." The verses run thus, each marked by a participial style in Hebrew (using RSV phrases for our English version):

> I. (4:13) "He who forms the mountains and creates the wind,
>   and declares to man what is his thought,
>   who makes the morning darkness
>   and treads upon the height of the earth —
>   Yahweh is his name!"

(Each stanza will end with a reference to the earth and with this refrain.)

> II. (5:8) "He who turns deep darkness into morning,
>   and deepens the day into night,
>   and calls forth the waters of the sea,
>   and pours them out on the surface of the earth —
>   Yahweh is his name!"

(5:9 is assumed to be an even later addition, different in content.)

> III. (9:5–6) "He who touches the earth, and it melts,
>   and all who dwell in it mourn,
>   who builds his upper chambers in the heavens,
>   and founds his vault upon the earth —
>   Yahweh is his name!"

(9:5b is a secondary addition, from 8:8.)

In Wolff's opinion such a hymn took shape in the preexilic period as part of Israel's controversy with the mythic beliefs of the ancient Near Eastern world. The hymn aimed to show God's activity in nature as well as in history. Who sends the wind and alternates day and night? None other than Yahweh. I add only two comments. Whatever we decide about the origin of these verses — by Amos, or a hymn he quotes, or hymnic fragments later inserted in his work — one thing that is clear is that Yahweh the creator is a god who keeps up his creative activity, night and day and in the life of man (4:13). Secondly his continuing activity includes judgment. Indeed, that note, that Yahweh can "melt the earth" and "make men mourn," is probably what caused it to be inserted in chapter 9, where the context is judgment and punishment for the "sinful kingdom" (9:8), Israel.

Our final example has to do with possible references in the prophets to that Israelite epic about Yahweh and the chaos monster which we have conjectured. We know the names given to this monster of watery chaos in neighboring lands: in Mesopotamia, Tiamat; at Ugarit, "Yam" (the sea) and "Nahar" (the river); in other texts, Leviathan (the coiled one) and Tannin (dragon). Now note some passages in the prophets where a battle between Yahweh and such a creature may be reflected:

> The Lord with his hard and great and strong sword will punish Leviathan the fleeing serpent, Leviathan the twisting serpent, and he will slay the dragon that is in the sea (Isaiah 27:1).

> Was thy wrath against the rivers, O Lord? . . .
>   or thy indignation against the sea? . . .
> the raging waters swept on;
>   the deep voice gave its voice,
>   it lifted up its hands on high.
> The sun and moon stood still . . .
>   at the light of thine arrows as they sped,
>   at the flash of thy glittering spear . . .
> Thou didst trample the sea with thy horses,
>   the surging of the mighty waves. (Habakkuk 3:8-15)

Jeremiah 5:22 may reflect Yahweh's conquest of the primordial sea monster when the prophet has God saying,

> I placed the sand as the bound for the sea,
> a perpetual barrier which it cannot pass;
> though the waves toss, they cannot prevail. . . .

A final case from Ezekiel: God says to Pharaoh, king of Egypt,

> . . . you are like a dragon in the seas. . . .
> I will throw my net over you. . . .
> I will haul you up in my dragnet.
> And I will cast you on the ground. . . .
> I will strew your flesh upon the mountains,
> and fill the valleys with your carcass.
> I will drench the land . . . with your flowing blood;
> and the watercourses will be full of you.
>   (Ezekiel 32:2-8, cf. 29:3-5)

The scene is similar to the one in *Enuma elish* where Marduk uses the carcass of Tiamat to fashion from it the world.[18]

There remains the curious detail that only in Old Testament poetry, and in texts dating from after the seventh century, the name "Rahab" is given to the creature vanquished by Yahweh in combat. Compare Job 9:13 or 26:12, or in the prophets, Isaiah 30:7 —

> Egypt's help is worthless and empty,
> therefore have I called her
> Rahab who sits still (RSV) — or, more likely (as in NEB and
> NAB), "Rahab quelled."

From such references there is a reasonable case for claiming that Israel knew a creation myth, even one where Yahweh bested a sea monster, and that the prophets occasionally reflect this epic (model two, in our presentation above).

It will also be observed, however, that (1) the biblical writers sometimes use this imagery to reflect political affairs ("Egypt is likened to the monster Rahab"); creation imagery thus is used in the service of historical reality. And when the prophets spoke about Yahweh defeating Rahab-Egypt, perhaps they had in mind that great victory of centuries before, which we call the exodus. (2) Note that often this chaos-battle imagery is transferred from the past, either at creation or the exodus, and placed in the future tense.

"*In that day* the Lord *will slay* the dragon that is in the sea." "I *will drench* the land with your blood." We are here on the verge of the apocalyptic mood, where creation-redemption was to take a new turn, in the hope for a "new creation."

B. The Psalms as Mirror of Creation and Its Continuance

Enough has already been said to make clear that the psalms of the temple and its cult were a natural place for creation emphases to burst forth. It was there in the ancient Near Eastern civilizations that creation was especially celebrated, in hymns and prayers: "Praise to the Creator!" *Enuma elish,* the Babylonian Genesis, ends in a hymn to Marduk, and the exuberant mood of praise for the deity, which we find in the psalms of Israel, also stands behind the Bible's affirmations about creation in Genesis 1 and 2. Hence the Psalter, stretching over many hundreds of years, includes hymns that speak of Yahweh's prowess and goodness in creating all things and continuing his care.[19]

The question we discussed in connection with the prophets, about the place of myth and to what extent there was Israelite acceptance of a chaos-battle involving Yahweh, again appears in connection with the psalms. The view we noted there, that Israelites sometimes absorbed into their view of Yahweh a notion of him as creator through a triumph over the monster of the deep at the dawn of time, has been applied even more widely in the psalms. We have already noted places where creation material from Egypt had been absorbed into a poem about Yahweh (Ps. 104).[20] How even more likely, proponents of this view hold, that cultic hymns should have accepted chaos-conflict views from the surrounding world.

However, there is by no means consensus on this issue, let alone on the existence of a full-fledged New Year's cult observance in Israel, with all the implications it had in Babylonia; indeed, some of the scholarly reconstructions of what the Babylonian festival was like have themselves been questioned![21] Samuel Terrien, in an examination of those psalms which seem at first most congenial to the theory of primordial battle with a chaos dragon and an emphasis on nature as the realm of Yahweh's working — namely, Psalms 74:12-17 ("thou didst crush the heads of Leviathan, thou didst give him as food for the creatures of the wilderness"); 89:5-12 ("thou didst crush Rahab like a carcass"); and 104:5-9 ("at thy rebuke" the waters fled) — Terrien concludes that even in these instances no cosmic battle is envisioned.[22] Further, he says, such psalms in Israel are not shaped only by cult practices but also by the faith of Israel. Indeed, Terrien holds, the aim is "not primarily to praise the Creator but to establish hymnically the omnipotence of the Lord of history." [23]

That last phrase raises again another issue with which we are by now familiar, that of "nature and history," "creation and redemption." Commentaries on the Psalms cannot help but face the question of which is primary. The fact of the matter is that the psalter is somewhat selective in its themes. Thus, there is little on the patriarchs; the Sinai tradition appears only modestly. The history-of-salvation is more prominent, usually in rather broad sweep (e.g., Pss. 78, 105, 106). And so, inevitably, creation, we have said, appears at times, as a theme in its own right — often, one is tempted to suggest, when reflections of general ancient Near Eastern thought are found (Pss. 104; 74:12-17, etc.) — and sometimes fused with other themes. Psalm 19, for instance, combines a hymn (19:1-6) on the creation theme ("The heavens are telling the glory of God . . ."), replete with mythological analogy (vv. 5-6, the skies are a race course where the sun runs a daily race), together with a poem about the law (19:7-14, "The law of the Lord is perfect, reviving the soul . . ."). Here, it can be argued, the two themes, perhaps once separate compositions, are brought together by the claim that Yahweh both creates the world and gives Israel the law; he is to be praised for both.[24]

But probably the most important observation as to themes in the psalter is to call attention to the emphasis on Israel — how the nation came into existence ("when God *created* Israel") and how God sustains her. Indeed, some of the references to "the world" are to be seen precisely in relation to Israel. Christoph Barth writes, "Even in His work of creation God is at work to bring into being the reality that is called 'Israel.'" Just as in the Yahwist's history, when he prefixed a creation account to the story of the patriarchs and then exodus, so in certain psalms the creation of the world is regarded "as being one stage in the creation of *Israel,*" and "the meaning of the history of the *world* is found in the history of *salvation.*[25] One may compare what we suggested with regard to 1 Corinthians 8:6 — in the plan of God the redeemed community holds a place with reference to the whole created world.

Thus, the Psalms do include the creation motif, sometimes right out of the thought-world of the day, with Egyptian or Mesopotamian modes of expression. But these emphases have been "Yahwehized," at least by the nature and heritage of the community that now recites them and more particularly by their being combined with other themes more characteristic of Israel's history and sometimes by being pruned, rewritten, or "demythologized."

One other observation is in order before citing an example or two from the Psalms. That is the fact that in the Psalms creation is, as elsewhere in the Old Testament, conceived of as a continuing process. Commenting on the way Psalm 24 describes the world in typical ancient Near Eastern fashion as a flat disc floating on the deep and supported by mountains that go down to the bottom of the sea, Helmer Ringgren relates this to the promise faith proclaims in Psalm 93:1 (and 96:10), "the world is established, it shall never be moved." He then goes on:

> the doctrine of creation is not primarily a theoretical statement about the origin of the world, about something that has happened long ago. It is rather a proclamation of a present reality; creation means that the evil powers are defeated, and that the order of the world is established for ever. That is what affords security to man as he lives in God's world. Creation, therefore, is also a redemptive act, the results of which are still present and form a constant source of joy and gratitude, especially on the occasions when they are commemorated in the cult.[26]

I pass over comment on his interesting observation that in the view of the chaos-battle myth "creation . . . is a redemptive act," in order to pursue Ringgren's main point, that God's creative activity continues. Ample illustrations can be provided from the Psalms, especially 104 with its emphasis that God provides water, food, regulation of time, and sustains all life —

When thou openest thy hand, they are filled with good things
(104:28). The intention, von Rad remarks, is "to show how the
whole world ... in every moment of its existence ... requires to be
sustained by God. ... Were Yahweh to turn away from the world
even for just one moment, then its splendor would immediately
collapse." [27] A stronger picture of continuing creation can scarcely
be imagined!

Enough has been said of creation in the Psalms generally. A few
actual passages may now be quoted. Psalm 89:5-13 deals with God's
wonders in creation, at times in almost pagan mythological language:

> Let the heavens praise thy wonders, O Lord.
>   [Then, after reference to his preeminence in the council of
>   the gods],
> Thou dost rule the raging of the sea ...
> Thou didst crush Rahab ...
> The heavens are thine, the earth also is thine,
>   the world and all that is in it, thou hast founded them.
> The north and the south, thou hast created them.

Yet all this creation-talk is set in the context of God's steadfast love
seen in history, to David and his house, experienced by the Israelites who sing his praise (89:1-4, 14ff.).

Psalm 8 celebrates God's glory revealed in his works in the
heavens and in the place of dominion he has given man on earth.
Note here the emphasis on man as crown of creation.

Psalm 74 recalls God's deeds in creation language — crushing
Leviathan, smiting the rivers, fixing the bounds of earth and of the
seasons. But this hymn refers to all this enumeration in vv. 12-17 as
"working *salvation* in the midst of the earth"; the term may mean
to recall Yahweh's creative work of salvation at the exodus, just as
the Psalm as a whole centers on God's people and their holy mount.

The mood in Psalm 74 is that of prayer and petition. That in 8
and 89 is admonition to praise. "How majestic is your name!"
"Praise Yahweh's wonders!" Creation, initial and continuing; Yahweh's redemptive acts; thanksgiving for all this forms the basis
for the Psalms' paean of praise.

C. Creation and Redemption in Deutero-Isaiah

Deutero-Isaiah or the Second Isaiah, as the "Great Unknown" who prophesied during the exile in Babylon and its dark days is known, is the most important voice to hear on the issue of how creation continued and took the shape of new redemptive acts. For Deutero-Isaiah has been claimed as the best illustration of the centrality of creation in the Old Testament and has even been credited with substituting "creation faith" for Israel's traditional message of the exodus as a basis for the new gospel he was commissioned to proclaim.[28] On the other hand, in spite of the many and lengthy creation-references in his words, he has been said by others still to fit within von Rad's dictum that creation in the Old Testament is never an independent doctrine but is always subservient to the redemption theme.[29] Isaiah chapters 40 and following are thus crucial for our investigation, and fortunately recent major examination of this material suggests a solution.[30]

First a word about this prophet and where he stands in the history of Israel. The man who has given his name to all sixty-six chapters of the Book of Isaiah, the original prophet Isaiah, was active in the second half of the eighth century B.C., his career coming to an end about a hundred years before the fall of Jerusalem. The first thirty-nine chapters of the book are generally traced to this prophet who flourished 742-687 B.C.

It was in 587/86 that Jerusalem fell and many of its inhabitants were carted off by their conquerors to live in exile by the waters of Babylon. They stayed there until an edict from the new Persian king, Cyrus, in 538 B.C. allowed some of the Jews to return to Jerusalem and even to begin rebuilding their temple and shattered religious life. It was during the most difficult decade or so of the Babylonian captivity, perhaps 550 to 538, after the first numbness of defeat wore off, before Cyrus arose, and when the temptation was greatest to grow slack and desert the faith, that one of the exiles arose and spoke words of encouragement.

This prophet's name has not been recorded. But he preached boldly, pastorally, majestically, and his words were so revered that in time they became attached to the scroll containing Isaiah 1-39. This was fitting, for in a sense the mantel of one of Israel's great prophets had fallen appropriately on the shoulders of this great unknown. Second or Deutero-Isaiah, as the critics call him, is represented to posterity by chapters 40-55 in our existing Book of Isaiah. (The remaining chapters in Isaiah, 56-66, are assigned to a still later prophetic figure, the Third Isaiah. We shall have occasion to refer to two key verses in his work in Section D below.)

The particular issue facing us in "The Book of Comfort," as Isaiah 40-55 has been referred to by some students of it, has already been outlined: the relation of the many creation-references to redemption. Isaiah's main message is clearly, of course, redemption, that God is going to do an unprecedented new thing, greater than the exodus from Egypt, comparable to creation itself; he will let his people return across a wondrous highway which is to appear, leveling the mountains and spanning valleys in the wilderness between Babylon and Jerusalem, and thus go home, to peace, security, and joy. God will restore, Jacob will return, and God's servant people will prosper in spite of vicissitudes. The redeemed of the Lord will break forth into a new song. This is the gospel of Deutero-Isaiah.

All these good tidings are told in a series of images, and again and again they employ and are undergirded by creation imagery. The God who speaks is "the Creator of the ends of the earth" (40:28). He speaks as the one "who created you, O Jacob, who formed you, O Israel" (43:1), "the Creator of Israel" (43:15). He is the Lord who "stretched out the heavens" and "spread out the earth" (44:24). God can say, echoing Genesis 1, "I form light" — and even "create darkness" (45:7). "He did not create the earth a chaos but formed it to be inhabited" (45:18). The chaos-battle myth can also be invoked; God is addressed with the words, "Was it not thou that didst cut Rahab in pieces, that didst pierce the dragon?" (51:9). What is the purpose of such extensive references to creation, which often seem to give the underlying support for hoping in what God is going to do in delivering his people again?

The answer of von Rad has already been given. He notes this juxtaposition of creation and redemption, but regards them as part of one divine plan of salvation.[31] (Here he reflects the viewpoint of heilsgeschichte.) Creation, in harmony with soteriology, is incorporated into the theme of redemption. Another German scholar[32] carried this view further by noting that the creation language in Deutero-Isaiah occurs primarily in statements by Yahweh himself, concerning his actions now or in the immediate future, soon to come to pass. The background, it is to be realized, lay in hymns from the Jerusalem temple, but the reference is no longer "proto-logical" (to the "first things" or the initial act of creating), but to the present, to creation which continues — in the form of new redemptive acts of God.

The alternative position [33] notes that Deutero-Isaiah stresses creation-faith in a way no previous prophetic figure ever had. Moreover, his statements are quite specific about creation-faith. At 45:11-13 God authenticates what he is going to do in raising up Cyrus as his "anointed one" by referring to belief in himself as creator. In chapter 40, verses 12-17, 21-24 set forth God's prowess in the world of nature in tandem with his coming acts in history which are described in the rest of the chapter. At 45:18 the description that Yahweh is creator is paralleled with the fact that he alone is God (in contrast to all the idols of the pagan world; cf. Deuteronomy 6:4).

In earlier times, the argument goes on, the exodus tradition might have been cited as the basis for believing in new redemptive acts on the part of God. But now God tells his people to forget such "former things" (43:18) and not remember how he had brought them through the sea to the promised land (43:16-17). Why forget what for hundreds of years had been the basic component in Israel's faith (though we have suggested that even in the crisis of the Yahwist's times, traditional emphases no longer carried the weight they once had)? The answer, it has been suggested, is that the old appeal to the exodus tradition no longer sufficed, either to convince the exiles about the power of God to work their rescue or because memories of the exodus by their ancestors so long before were not adequate to support the "new things" to be believed. Deutero-Isaiah is thus understood to be filling in a gap, caused by the collapse of old traditions, by appealing now to something more tangible, the creation which one could see all about him, even (or especially) in Babylon. "Creation faith" in this way would replace the gospel of the exodus redemption as the means for making credible the new promises of God.

A word must be inserted at this point about the prominence of the creation theme in Babylon. For the Jews in captivity there, the mythology and ritual of creation had taken on a significance it never had at Jerusalem, even if we grant some sort of new year's festival at the temple before its destruction in 586, and all the creation emphasis which accompanied such a festival. Babylon was, after all, the home of the creation-battle epic, *Enuma elish.* Here there were magnificent processions along the *via sacra* or sacred way, through the Ishtar Gate, across the Euphrates, to the *akitu* hut, and then with great rejoicing back to Babylon and the other temple cities. We must imagine the importance which creation took on for Jews as they watched the pomp and processionals of this twelve-day festival each year, when Marduk was enthroned as king and the chaos-battle ritually reenacted. While one reaction on the part of Jews would have been to dismiss the idols in it as "molten images" and "things of nothingness" (40:18-20, etc.), another response was surely to claim similar grandeur for Yahweh as creator too. Thus the creation-references in Deutero-Isaiah are almost inevitable, given this situation.

We now have some idea of the problems which the great unknown prophet faced, and have set forth the issue of the relation of his creation-references to his message of redemption. How, precisely, did he proceed to let faith speak in Babylon, so that creation might continue in the form of a new redemptive exodus? A recent study of Deutero-Isaiah by Carroll Stuhlmueller [34] makes clear that the prophet grasped hold of every literary form and theme of content he could find to get his message across.

In terms of forms, the prophet used types of speech familiar to his people from the now-destroyed temple in Jerusalem, from prophets of the past, and from daily life. Thus, for example, he employed the kind of disputation form, full of questions, which one might hear in the market place (40:12-31, "Who has measured the waters in the hollow of his hands . . . ?"), or the sort of judgment speech heard in a law court ("Listen to me, . . . let us draw near for judgment . . . ," 41:1ff.).

More significantly, Deutero-Isaiah employed forms familiar from temple worship. One illustration is the "oracle of salvation" from God, a form consisting of (1) a salutation to the abject worshiper,

(2) an expression of encouragement, (3) the reason for that encouragement, and (4) the result and (5) the goal of Yahweh's coming intervention, all in response to some prayer of lament. As an example, compare 41:8-13:

(1) salutation or address — vv. 8-9, spoken to God's servant, Jacob or Israel:
(2) the words of encouragement — 10a, "Do not fear," a traditional wording;
(3) the basis of encouragement — 10b, "I am with you . . . , I am your God."

Then comes (4) the result of Yahweh's work: vv. 11-12, enemies will perish; and (5) the goal, v. 13, "I, Yahweh, hold your right hand," and the encouragement is repeated.

Just to hear the form is like having a comforting recollection from childhood; it is familiar to the Judeans in exile. The most important temple form which the prophet reflects is the hymn, for example at 45:8 and 54:1-3; by echoing strains of hymnic praise they had known in Jerusalem, Deutero-Isaiah could help revive the hopes of the exiles to return again and praise Yahweh there.

His themes too sometimes come from Israel's past. At times Second Isaiah refers to the exodus tradition. The passage at 40:3-11 describes a journey through the wilderness; 43:1-7 talks of passing through the waters; 43:16-17 alludes to the first exodus, in preparation for a new one from Babylon. The prophet can also appeal to the traditional theme of election: Yahweh had in the past chosen the children of Israel and the house of David; 44:1-5 picks up that theme. The idea of God as *go'el* or redeemer, who redeemed his people, a powerful image from the past, continues too (e.g., 43:1-7; 54:1-10). But creation ideas are also invoked: the chaos-battle at 51:9-10; and the image, familiar especially in Babylon, of a sacred procession, at 52:7-10; indeed, the whole picture in 40:3ff., of the return to Zion through the wilderness, can be interpreted as a massive Israelite version of a Babylonian parade along the sacred way!

Now that we have seen how the prophet employed forms and themes of all sorts from his world, we turn to the main question: plainly Deutero-Isaiah uses creation themes — but how? Stuhlmueller concludes with a surprising answer: Isaiah employs them "redemptively." His exact term to describe Isaiah's work is "creative redemption"; that, he says, is *the* theme in the Great Unknown. It is not that creation has replaced redemption, or that creation is a once-upon-a-time action by God in the past; rather creation thought is a way of expressing God's redemptive power now. As Stuhlmueller defines it, creation means "a wondrous . . . act of Yahweh" now — a "redemptive" act, "bringing to Israel a new national existence and a new prosperity of unprecedented scope, with 'creative' repercussions upon all the elements of Israel's existence, even upon the cosmos." [35]

Does Deutero-Isaiah employ references to the first creation as *proof* for what God is going to do? No, Stuhlmueller thinks, for the prophet never argues *from* creation but refers to it only incidentally, evocatively. What he does stress is Yahweh's *present* creating, his continuing redemptive power. But that is the matter of his lordship, creative-redemptively.

Does the prophet go so far as to see the whole cosmos affected by God's creative-redemption for Israel? There are passages which hint at nature being transformed — hills are flattened, valleys filled in, the wilderness blossoms like a garden — but all this, we must observe, is for Israel's sake in her historic trek homewards. The most universal reference is at 45:8 where all of heaven and earth are to participate in a new creation.[36] But generally the focus is on Israel.

Thus, Deutero-Isaiah presents us with the most massive and amazing use of creation language in the entire Bible. But the primary purpose of it all is to get across a message of redemption. Creation is one theme among many used to present the new exodus. It is a significant theme, no doubt of that, but refers to creation as it continues in Israel's life preeminently; and that, in the form of a new redemptive act. We are on the verge — though Deutero-Isaiah does not use the word — of "new creation" as a concept.

Did it all work out as Deutero-Isaiah hoped? History records that Cyrus, the Persian king hailed as "messiah" (44:28; 45:1ff.), did let some of the Jews return home. But the road back was rocky and stony, not miraculous. Acacia, myrtle, and olive trees (41:19) did not automatically spring up in the desert west of Babylon. The temple the returnees were able to build was a miserable affair, and God had to raise up new prophets later on. But Second Isaiah's words fulfilled a purpose for their day and have brought hope to countless hearts ever since, even if not everything was carried out literally.

We note: in concluding our discussion, one feature in Second Isaiah not always observed: in his imagery and hopes for the future he was close to the apocalyptists and their dreams. Indeed he has been called "the father of apocalyptic." [37] As a postscript on the Isaianic story and as a link to our final chapter on the "new creation" in the New Testament, we add a word about two verses in Third Isaiah.

D. Toward New Creation: Third Isaiah

Disciples and successors of the Great Unknown continued to prophesy in the wretched times which followed the return from Babylon to Palestine. Sayings, oracles, promises, and psalms from various hands have been collected and attached to our Book of Isaiah as chapters 56 to 66. The nucleus of this material, consisting of chapters 60-62 plus sections of 65 and other chapters, is attributed to a prophet between the years 537 and 515 to whom the name "Trito-Isaiah" or Third Isaiah is given. The exact origin of other units in these chapters is very hard to trace, and some sections are no doubt much later. [38]

The situation these spokesmen for God faced was a gloomy and discouraging one. In contrast to what the returning Israelites had hoped for, existence was precarious, work on the temple went slowly, enemies harassed them on every side, faith drooped to low ebb. The prophets of this period still used some of the forms and themes enunciated by Deutero-Isaiah, but because of the dark times they were led more and more to apocalyptic outlook and mood of mind. That term "apocalyptic" implies that things were bad, so bad, that it will take an intervention by God to set them right. Hope rests not in human achievement but solely on what God will do by his miraculous intervention. [39]

A typical oracle by Third Isaiah for such times is that at 65:16*b*-25. The prophet contrasts "former troubles" (16*b*) with the great salvation to come (vv. 17-25). His announcement about what God is going to do ran something like this:[40]

18a   Be glad and rejoice for ever
        over that which I create,
16b   because former troubles are forgotten
        and are hid from my eyes.
17   For behold, I create new heavens and a new earth,
        and the former things shall not be remembered or come
            to mind.
18b   For behold, I create Jerusalem a rejoicing,
        and her people a joy.
19   I will rejoice in Jerusalem
        and be glad in my people.

Verses 19b-24 then describe this good time to come, in terms of no more weeping (v. 19b), no premature death (20) or pointless work wiped out by catastrophes (21-23), and with the promise that those blessed by Yahweh will have access to him (23b-24). Verse 25, which describes how even the animals will dwell in peace, the wolf lying down with the lamb, may be a later addition, based upon Isaiah 11:6-9, but it introduces an important principle: the great time to come when Yahweh changes things will be like the golden age of creation when he first made the world (in a famous formula, *"Endzeit gleicht Urzeit,"* eschatology will recapitulate protology).[41] Verse 25 hints, as we have seen in other texts, that God's redemptive actions on behalf of Israel will have repercussions in the whole realm of nature.

The phrase with which verse 17 begins encapsules this broad hope in what was to become the classic phrase: "I create new heavens and a new earth." This is the first time the words "new heavens and new earth" are found in the Bible. They may well have sprung up in apocalyptic circles which held the existing world to be so bad that only a new universe would do, or at least a divine renovation of man's world was needed. Such sweeping change will be like the initial creation itself. Indeed, the very verb used for "create" is that which the Priestly writer employed *(bara')* in Genesis 1 for God's creating there.

But if this apocalyptic vision here quoted of a new creation had in itself universal implications, the prophet in Isaiah 65 has given it a much more specific meaning. For Third Isaiah here understands "the new heavens and new earth" to refer to the transformation which is to come upon the people of Israel and specifically Jerusalem. Note the precise parallelism;

65:17 "For behold, I create new heavens and a new earth";
65:18 "For behold, I create Jerusalem a rejoicing,
          and her people a joy."

The new creation has to do with the people of Israel, specifically their city of Jerusalem, and every verse which follows deals with the people of Jerusalem ("my people . . . , they [in Jerusalem]," vv. 20-24). Even in verse 25, with its hint of nature being affected, the final note is of Yahweh's "holy mount," the hill of the temple, Zion. So the apocalyptic phrase here, about the new heavens and new earth, turns out really to refer to people, transformed, under God, God's people, the faithful in Israel.

How attractive this image of new heavens and earth was to be is shown by one final reference at Isaiah 66:22. Here an even later prophetic voice, quite definitely under the spell of apocalyptic, speaks of a time when all the pagan nations will respond to messengers sent to them, and will declare Yahweh's glory and even be admitted to this priesthood (66:18-19, 21, in prose in the RSV).[42] Some less liberal spoilsport seems to have found those sentiments too radical, and so tacked on verses 20, 22-24 as a corrective — the movement, he insists, will not be *to* the nations to save them, but *from* the nations as Jewish exiles come home, released from their Gentile captivity (v. 20), to engage in eternal worship (v. 23) and even, as often in apocalyptic, a little gloating over the fate of the wicked (v. 24). (That's one trouble with apocalyptic voices: one sometimes counterbalances the other; and the pessimistic situation leads to either excessive optimism or overharsh zeal against enemies. It is Jewish custom never to end the Book of Isaiah on verse 24 and its note of doom, but to read verse 23 as the final word.)

In this complex of 66:18-24 what interests us is the basis offered to ground the visions that have been sketched. What provides the evidence for the hope that is voiced? Nothing other than the promise of new heavens and a new earth, already known in the writer's circle —

> For as the new heavens and the new earth which I will make
>   shall remain before me, says Yahweh,
> so shall your descendants and your name remain. . . .
> All flesh shall come to worship before me.

Promises are based on promises.

Once the basis for anticipating new acts of God had been the experience of the exodus. In Deutero-Isaiah it sometimes became creation that provided that basis — not the original creation but God's continuing creative work, which may express itself as redemption in the present. Here in Isaiah 66 continuing creation has been extended forward to the end of time, when it promises to take the form of a new creation. That was a category for the followers of Jesus Christ to conjure with.

IV

New Creation—
Hope and
New Existence Now

Early Christianity, no matter where we lay hold of it, thought itself caught up in something new.[1]

During the ministry of Jesus, the prophet from Nazareth attracted followers precisely because he announced that the long-awaited kingdom of God was at hand, and his words and deeds, parables and miracles, promises and demands anticipated the coming of this new stage in the program of God.

After the resurrection, as the disciples became apostles and went about announcing how God had raised Jesus from the dead and made him lord, the emphasis was on a new "way," a way of access to God, a way of life with one another, a way of hope for the future. Eventually a new community, the church, evolved.

Again and again in this community of Jesus Christ the adjective "new" is heard, even as the age-old Hebrew scriptures and their contents are carried over and treasured: a new covenant (from Jeremiah 31, but now realized in Jesus' death); a new commandment (radicalizing and epitomizing the ancient will of God from the beginning); new life, the life of the new age, about which apocalyptists had dreamed; and the new man, as Paul and his successors were to call the species of humanity taking shape under the lordship of Jesus Christ.

In many ways the most striking phrase for summing up all this is "the new creation." It forms the subject of this chapter, in the two particular forms which we encounter in the New Testament and which need to be explored: the "new heavens and new earth," a phrase from the Old Testament which is carried over into the Christian scriptures at several points; and the "new creation" of which Paul speaks.

To concentrate thus on new creation is not to shortchange the views found in the New Testament on original and continuing creation, but simply to concentrate on what is novel and most significant. Moreover, we have already explored one early Christian formula about creation, initial and continuing, at 1 Corinthians 8:6, and have referred to others at Colossians 1:15-20 and more briefly at Hebrews 1:2-3, John 1:1ff., and elsewhere.[2] In even those few examples we have seen how there are many similarities between New Testament talk of creation and the statements in the Old Testament: in both instances it is faith that speaks, claiming for God the role as creator at the beginning and since then as sustainer of life, using terms and forms and ideas from the world of the day. The chief difference is, of course, that the New Testament gives Jesus Christ a place in this, as agent or mediator of the creation.

It would be interesting to explore additional New Testament statements about creation, but little would be added except to show the vigor and variety of how Christianity spoke of the Lord Jesus Christ, and how quickly and widespread this acclamation of him as creating as well as redeeming grew up. Indeed, very early, when Hellenistic Jewish Christians began to preach to people outside Palestine, the theme of creation came to be attached to the apostolic kerygma about Jesus' death and resurrection, and thence it spread in creed and faith.[3]

Let it suffice here to call attention to the forms and functions assumed by the several New Testament statements on creation. 1 Corinthians 8:6 represents a creed. John 1 and Colossians 1 reflect early Christian hymns. The creation imagery could be employed in ethical appeals (recall 1 Corinthians 10:26 or compare 2 Corinthians 9:7-12 or 1 Peter 4:19), or in connection with baptism (Colossians 3:10 and Ephesians 2:10, involving the "image of God" given "in Christ"; and, I think, James 1:18, where the "begetting by the word of truth" as "a kind of first fruits of God's creation" seems to refer to rebirth by baptism), or, very interestingly, in describing man's situation before God as sinner and as God's child

(Romans 1 and 5; John 3). It is the apocalyptic application of creation themes that will occupy us especially, however.

A. The New Heavens and the New Earth — Christian Style

The dark times which Second and Third Isaiah addressed in the sixth and fifth centuries B.C. did not depart for most Jews in the years toward the close of what we call the Old Testament era and the ensuing Intertestamental Period. Crisis followed crisis, disaster came upon disaster, one conqueror left the stage of history and another came. Hence pious circles in Israel had good reason to cling to future apocalyptic hopes, because the present was so bad. Apocalyptic expectations cry out in document after document which we have not time to explore here. The idea of a "renewal of the world" by Yahweh's action became a commonplace.[4]

Inevitably such apocalyptic ideas played a role in primitive Christianity too. To what extent Jesus himself expected the coming Son of man or the consummation of history in his own lifetime, and the question of how pervasive the hope for the parousia was in the first-century church continue to be debated.[5] Certain it is that the New Testament documents refer to such things, and some Christians were apocalyptists. That this sort of apocalyptic hope was the matrix for the entire Christian movement and its theology has been claimed.[6] In any case, whenever someone in a Jewish context announced that a person had been raised from the dead, as Jesus was, it inevitably set in motion ideas of the last times and sent hearers racing to apocalyptic texts and promises.

There is no question but that Jewish writings of an apocalyptic stamp were treasured in early Christianity. The Book of Isaiah — First, Second, and Third Isaiahs included — was, of course, a favorite. So were some of the noncanonical writings from the Intertestamental Period alluded to above. We therefore have every right to expect phrases and ideas from Jewish writings of this sort to crop up in the New Testament.[7]

We probably err, however, if we assume these apocalyptic reflections showed a steady curve of interest, either beginning with an intense early apocalypticism which then cooled, or commencing from a non-apocalyptic Jesus and mounting steadily. On the contrary, the fever chart of apocalypticism no doubt rose and fell repeatedly as circumstances changed, and it may well have varied from one locality to another. Therefore it is important to try to set each instance of "end-time language" [8] in its specific situation. *Why did a writer invoke this way of talking about God?*

In the case of the seer who wrote the Apocalypse of John about A.D. 95 we have a rather clear idea of the situation he faced. John composed his amazing document, with its letters to the seven churches of Asia Minor, the series of visions, and hopeful promises, at a time when the future of Christianity seemed dark. Persecution was arising, from local opposition, and more significantly from the rulers of the empire: because Christians could and would not engage in worship of the emperor Domitian as lord and god, they faced the threat of government suppression. As in the times of the Second and Third Isaiahs, the faithful must have been tempted to compromise or abandon what they had believed when they came to faith.

John's apocalypse appeals to Christians to hang on. He holds out the expectation that God will soon intervene. He promises deliverance and a great time coming, as well as destruction of enemies and vengeance on Rome. All this is typical of apocalyptic literature, and is presented with the usual devices of that medium — sights, sounds, colors, trumpets, smells, yells, visions, angels, voices, and symbolic happenings.[9] It is likely that John employed all sorts of sources available from the Old Testament, later Jewish writings, ancient oriental myths, and the Roman world of the day. A particularly Christian feature throughout the work is the use of the adjective "new" in connection with what has come to pass in Jesus Christ. John's apocalypse speaks of a new name (2:17), a new song (5:9; 14:3), the new Jerusalem (3:12; 21:2) — and "a new heaven and a new earth" (21:1). We shall concentrate on the passage where this phrase from Trito-Isaiah appears.

Revelation 21:1ff. begins a magnificent vision meant to encourage the persecuted Christians with a picture of the new Jerusalem to come. Christians recognized Jerusalem, just as the ancient Israelites did, as their mother-city or metropolis, though at times they de-actualized this as "the Jerusalem above" and not the city in Judah (cf. Galatians 4:25-26). Here in chapter 21 the seer has constructed a poem of some six stanzas describing in glowing terms what the new Jerusalem will be like.[10] Listen to it especially for reflections of Isaianic imagery and the notion that the Final Time to come will be like that First Time when God created the heavens and the earth (italics indicate phrases from Isaiah):

> 21:5a And he who sat upon the throne said,
> 4d *"The former things* have passed away,
> (Isa. 43:18; 65:17*b*)
> 5b *Behold, I make* all things *new."* (Isa. 43:19)

I 21:1 And I saw *a new heaven and a new earth.*
(Isa. 65:17; 66:22)
For the first heaven and the first earth had passed away,
And the sea was no more.

II 21:2 And I saw *the holy city,* new *Jerusalem* (Isa. 52:1)
Coming down out of heaven from God,
Prepared *as a bride adorned* for her husband.
(Isa. 61:10)

III 21:3 And I heard a great voice from the throne saying,
"Behold, the dwelling of God is with men.
He will dwell with them,
And they will be his people,
And God himself will be with them.

IV 21:4 *"He will wipe away every tear from* their eyes,
(Isa. 25:8)
And *death* shall be *no more,* (Isa. 25:8; cf. 65:20)
Neither shall there be *mourning* nor *crying* nor *pain*
any more. (Isa. 35:10; 51:11; 65:19)
22:3 There shall be no more of anything accursed.

V 22:3 "And the throne of God and of the Lamb shall be in it
[Jerusalem],
And his servants shall worship him,
22:4 And they shall see his face,
And his name shall be on their foreheads.

VI 22:5 "And night shall be no more,
They will have no need of light of lamp or *light of sun,*
(Isa. 60:19)
For the Lord God will be their light,
And they shall reign for ever."

As we have reconstructed this poetic vision, it is replete with images especially from Isaiah 65, and also includes, in typical oriental style, seven things which will be "no more," on that great day to come; no more sea (21:1), or death, grief, crying, pain (21:4), accursed things (22:3), or night (22:5). Positively, the seer promises light, kingship (22:5), eternal fellowship with God (21:3; 22:3-4), and everlasting worship (22:3).[11]

Clearly, the author has begun with the universalistic phrase of Trito-Isaiah, "new heavens and earth," but how has he understood it? We must ask not merely what the tradition is which he takes over but how the biblical writer interprets it. Just as in Isaiah 65, that cosmic phrase has been interpreted to mean a new Jerusalem, a city for the redeemed of God. The view is likely correct that this city is not the old Jerusalem transformed, or the millennial city mentioned at 20:9ff., but a preexistent entity which comes down from above.[12] That is a change from Isaiah 65, but John 21 shares with Isaiah 65:17ff. the view that what the "new heavens and new earth" are about is a place for the redeemed, in this case the Christian faithful pressured by persecution on earth. To this extent the apocalyptic hope becomes focused, not on the cosmos or nature, but on the followers of the Lamb who keep the faith. Creation/new creation imagery thus serves redemption. The language of apocalyptic is a word of hope.

The phrase with which we are concerned crops up in one other New Testament document, the one critics believe to be the last book written in the entire canon, 2 Peter.[13] At 2 Peter 3:8ff. the author is setting forth a defense of the expectation that the Day of the Lord will surely come sometime. He defends this proposition against gnosticizing opponents who so emphasized the aspect of present fulfillment in Christianity that any future element was lost. In presenting his own views our orthodox writer invokes scripture (Psalm 90:4 is cited at 3:8, to explain the delay) and provides a picture of the destruction which will come upon the existing world — it will be destruction by fire (vv. 10, 12), a world conflagration such as was taught also by Stoics and in the Intertestamental literature.

The entire section is employed to set forth an ethical appeal for "holiness and godliness" (3:11, cf. 14ff.), which, if anything, will hasten the time of the end. The paragraph about the melting of the heavens with fire then closes with a promise (3:13): "according to God's promise we wait for new heavens and a new earth in which righteousness dwells." This righteousness is not the redeeming, delivering action of God, of which Isaiah and Paul speak, but justice, of which the existing world is so devoid.[14] In 2 Peter the promised "home of justice" (NEB) is a stage on which the just will be delivered from their enemies and rewarded for their good deeds (2 Peter 1:4ff.).

This use of "new heavens and new earth" in 2 Peter is reminiscent of the one noted at Isaiah 66:22 in that the grandiose cosmological concept serves really as scaffolding or support for the future life of the redeemed.[15] Apocalyptic thus employed the promise of such a new creation in order to arm believers for endurance in the time of crisis. There is little attention in such passages to the implications for the cosmos (perhaps only in Isaiah 65:25; in the Apocalypse of John the focus can scarcely be said to be directed on the non-Christian world; what counts is the little island of the faithful persecuted in Asia Minor). Therefore the apocalyptic use of its own phrase "new heavens and earth" turns out to be surprisingly "church-" or "Israel-centered."

B. The "New Creation" in Paul

Creation and even new creation have not always received high priority in treatments of the thought of the Apostle Paul. The latter, eschatological concept has probably fared better than the former in handbooks on the Apostle to the Gentiles. All too often what interest there is in creation in Paul may simply reflect attempts to make Paul fit later dogmatic outlines more than a concern for what he says in its own right. Thus creation as a Pauline concept has often been shunted aside as mere background for his chiefer themes, the righteousness of God, reconciliation, mystical union "in Christ," or "God's plan of salvation.[16] "New creation," as we have seen in Chapter I, has attracted more attention in recent years, but often as a slogan for either existential presentations of what the man in Christ is like or rapprochement with nature and a universal hope and cosmic Christology. What is really Paul's own view?

The apostle, writing in only the third decade of the existence of the Christian movement, to mission communities, in letters the agenda for which were set by the pressing needs of the moment, scarcely found opportunity to delve into speculation about "the beginning" or about "continuing creation." What is more, his eschatological expectation of the imminent end, during his life-time or shortly thereafter — and I doubt that Paul ever set aside the hope of Christ's parousia as a "mistaken notion" of his younger days which "mature insight" banished [17] — his expectation of the imminent end scarcely made consideration of creation likely either. When one expects the consummation any day, the present creation is not of such great import. When the decisive event has happened, in Jesus and his cross, and the parousia beckons, then what moment is there to discuss how this dying world began?

Yet Paul inherited, as a Jew, all of the thinking on creation which the writers of the Hebrew scriptures had done over the centuries. In particular, he was aware of the flood of ideas poured forth in the Intertestamental Period when "ktisiology" [18] or the doctrine of creation became a more major factor than it had been in Old Testa-ment times. We cannot pause to analyze the documents in the Apocrypha and Pseudepigrapha and Qumram or the rabbinical sources for what they have to say on creation. [19] But Saul of Tarsus no doubt was acquainted with these from the days before he became a follower and missionary of Jesus Christ on Damascus Road. Moreover, Paul lived in a world of "gods many and lords many," where Greco-Roman and Mediterranean cultures promul-gated a host of creation theories. [20]

Most important of all, we have already seen that Paul inherited from the Christian community affirmations on God's creation and the role of Jesus in it. 1 Corinthians 8:6 was the particular exam-ple discussed. [21] Another such confessional slogan is probably em-bedded at Romans 4:17, professing faith in God

who gives life to the dead

and calls into existence the things that do not exist.

In this case the belief in "creation out of nothing" *(creatio ex nihilo)* which had found expression among Jews first in the Intertestamental

Period (cf. 2 Maccabees 7:28), is set alongside confession of the resurrection as a similarly miraculous expression of the power of God.

It would be possible to list other instances where Paul cites material which speaks in creation language or where in his own right he mentions creation themes. His references to Adam and to Christ as the last Adam, in 1 Corinthians 15 and Romans 5, particularly deserve exploration, as do possible allusions to cosmic implications of the Christ event (Romans 8 will be discussed below). We shall concentrate, however, on the "new creation" passages, bearing in mind that Paul knew of various views on creation, biblical and otherwise; the Intertestamental extrapolations and emphases on ktisiology and also the problem of sin in God's creation [22]; and the early Christian acclamation of Jesus Christ as agent in creation and its continuing, especially as expressed in brief creeds and enthusiastic hymns of Hellenistic believers.

If any single passage dare be selected to typify Pauline use of creation imagery, it is probably 2 Corinthians 4:6, where God's words in the creation story at Genesis 1:3 are actually quoted: Paul claims, with reference to his own conversion, apostleship, and preaching, that

> it is the God who said, "Let light shine out of darkness," who has shone in our hearts to give the light of the knowledge of the glory of God in the face of Jesus Christ.

Creation is here the category which leaps into Paul's mind as analogy to what has happened to him in becoming Christian. It describes his redemption. Is this a clue to how he will understand the phrase "new creation"?

In approaching the Pauline phrase "new creation" *(kainē ktisis)* at Galatians 6:15 and 2 Corinthians 5:17, the investigator finds all sorts of pitfalls confronting him. Shall we render the adjective *kainē* as "new in time," "new in kind," or "renovated"? The Greek word means "new," and an older attempt to make a distinction between it and another Greek word *neos* as to the kind of newness — in time or in kind — does not hold up, as Roy Harrisville has shown.[23] But all the above renderings have been proposed. Next, does the noun *ktisis* mean "creation" or "creature"? Specifically does it refer to the creatures who make up the Christian community, or the whole human race; or all creation, including inanimate nonhuman things, what we call "nature"? Again various answers have been given, and our standard English translations in some instances reflect this perplexity by giving one rendering on the page and an alternate in a footnote. That is the case with 2 Corinthians 5:17 in the RSV, which renders it "new creation" but adds in a note "Or *creature.*" [24]

The fact of the matter is that the word *ktisis* probably has different meanings in different passages. At Colossians 1:23 it obviously means "creature" in the sense of every human being under heaven to whom the gospel is proclaimed. At Mark 10:6 it refers to "the beginning of creation." At Romans 1:25 it is rendered creature but takes in more than human creation, for animals are involved too. The standard lexicon on New Testament Greek offers a split verdict when it takes 2 Corinthians 5:17 to mean "a new creature" (as in the RSV note) but prefers "new creation" at Galatians 6:15.[25] The neuralgic passage which everyone debates is Romans 8:19-22: the whole creation that groans awaiting redemption includes all men, but does it also cover animals and inorganic creation? Is it only humanity that longs for the unveiling of the sons of God, or do trees, lakes, "rocks, rills, and templed hills" look with expectancy too? More on that when Romans 8, as our final passage, is discussed.

Any analysis of new creation in Paul runs into certain hazards and options reflected in the three approaches taken in three recent treatments of the topic. One of these involves the tendency, and shows the dangers, of using later dogmatic categories for analyzing Paul. The approach is exemplified in the book by Louis H. Taylor, published in 1958, *The New Creation: A Study of the Pauline Doctrines of Creation, Innocence, Sin, and Redemption.*[26] Dr. Taylor takes the commendable step of setting Paul's teaching on the new creation in an overall outline of the apostle's thought. He is, in my opinion, basically correct in seeing the new creation in Paul as primarily deliverance and salvation with reference to man; any effects on "the sub-human creation," as Taylor calls it, are put off till the age to come. Taylor's rendering of *kainē ktisis* as "renovated creation" may be debated, but the point where he is most to be questioned lies in the imposition of later dogmatic categories on the thought of Paul; for example, in the way this revision of a dissertation at the Southern Baptist Seminary, Louisville, Kentucky, struggles to show Paul taught men were innocent until they reach the age of reason and accountability. We must be careful not to read our later patterns and interests into Paul.

A very different approach is taken by Heinz Schwantes in a dissertation at Jena University, in East Germany, published in 1963 as *Schöpfung der Endzeit.*[27] What is the "creation of the last times," of which his title speaks? In Schwantes's opinion the new eschatological creation is nothing other than the resurrection, for the resurrection of Jesus Christ is what creates the new Adam, the new man. Resurrection is thus new creation in Christ. The verse to which Schwantes especially appeals is Romans 4:17, about "the God . . . who gives life to the dead and calls into existence the things that do not exist." Here resurrection and *creatio ex nihilo* (creation out of "things that do not exist") are paralleled as equally miraculous. Schwantes has recovered a valid Pauline emphasis. Resurrection, conversion, coming to be "in Christ" are nothing less than like the day when God said, "Let light shine out of darkness" (Genesis 1:3; 2 Corinthians 4:6). One must also be appreciative of the careful analysis of vocabulary in this study, on the basis of which Schwantes is able to claim that Paul used "creation vocabulary" much more sparingly than the literature of late Judaism did. I am also sensitive to his insistence that Paul's category of creation-resurrection brings something truly new, and not just a recapitulation of what had been at the beginning of the world. "Endzeit" is more than "Urzeit." But the insight that new eschatological creation relates to resurrection does not seem to exhaust all that there is in Paul.

The most recent approach that is relevant is found in the Princeton dissertation and its book form (1971) by John G. Gibbs, *Creation and Redemption: A Study in Pauline Theology.*[28] While Gibbs does not specifically discuss "new creation," focusing instead on the terms in his title and the modern debate over whether creation or redemption is basic, he is very much aware of recent discussions on "cosmic Christology" [29] and proposes that the theme of Christ's lordship be the central element in Pauline thought, spanning both creation and redemption. For 1 Corinthians 8:6 and other passages the formula would then be:

L (Lordship of Christ)

over both   Creation (C)   and   Redemption (R).

That is surely the way faith sees it, but is there any truth in the
formula for the world which does not confess Christ? That is, can
one come to picture Christ as lord of creation without first having
experienced the redemption which he mediates? [30] It seems significant, in my mind, that in order to make his case, Gibbs must
argue that the "theology of the cross" in Paul is not at the center
of his theology but is something peripheral. For Gibbs, "cosmic
Christology" is as central in Paul as the *theologia crucis* (the message about "Christ crucified upon the cross," 1 Corinthians 1:23)!
But is it? If so, we must ask, where does such a notion occur in
Paul's writings? Is it characteristic of Paul himself? A particular
failing in the dissertation, only partially remedied in its published
form, is lack of differentiation among pre-Pauline forms which the
apostle inherits, Paul's own thought (often seen in corrections he
makes in these formulas), and the later Deutero-Pauline literature.[31]

My judgment is that we can learn from all these approaches but
need to be aware of the problems they suggest.

To turn now to the two Pauline verses where "new creation" or
"new creature" occurs, we come to a solution, in my opinion,
precisely in light of the history-of-religions background we select.
For three different history-of-religions backgrounds have been
projected for the Pauline phrase *kainē ktisis*. We shall note the
pertinent verses in Paul; outline the background theories; and then
make a choice, in order to get at the meaning of each verse.

The Letter to the Galatians, written between A.D. 53 and 55 most
likely, reads at 6:15, three verses from the end of the epistle, in the
postscript presumably penned in the apostle's own hand: "Neither
circumcision counts for anything, nor uncircumcision, but a *kainē
ktisis*" (for the time being we may leave the key phrase untrans-
lated). 2 Corinthians 5 belongs to a letter that Paul wrote in 54 or
55. The verse using the phrase at 5:17 stands just before the famous
section on God's work of reconciliation: "Therefore, if anyone [is] in
Christ, *kainē ktisis!* The old has passed away, behold the new has
come. All this is from God who through Christ reconciled us. . . ."

(1) One theory as to where Paul got this expression "new crea-ture" or "creation" invokes the Old Testament prophets. Passages can be cited from the prophets, referring to the expectation of a new heart and a new spirit, so that the recipient will walk in Yahweh's statutes; cf. Jeremiah 31:33f.; Ezekiel 36:26f. The empha-sis in light of such passages has then been placed by commentators on the ethical implications and upon religious inwardness. Gerhard Schneider's study, *Kaine Ktisis* favors this background; [32] E. D. Burton, in his commentary, sees the result as "divine activity in the production of a new moral life," with a "radical transformation of character." [33] Few commentators, however, have been content to leave the matter on the level of the prophets and the moral life, so far as Paul's full meaning goes.

(2) The old treatment of Galatians by J. B. Lightfoot in 1865 proposed another background, one from the rabbis. [34] When a pros-elyte or Gentile convert to Judaism was baptized, the rabbis some-times referred to him as a "new creature" *(b*e*riyah h*a*dasah),* since his old world of associations was understood to have passed away. The convert now stands in a new relationship with God and with the community of Israel. Paul, against his rabbinic background, it is claimed, could quite naturally have used that phrase for a baptized Christian. Hence, to put 2 Corinthians 5:17 into rabbinic terms, "If any one is *en Christō,* he is *b*e*riyah h*a*dasah* — a new creature." It is not circumcision or the lack of it that matters, but new creaturehood. I personally find this explanation most attrac-tive, and experts on the Jewish roots of Christianity like Joachim Jeremias and W. D. Davies favor it. [35] Against it, however, are the facts that we do not know as much about the practice of proselyte baptism as we would like, and the texts from rabbinic sources using the phrase are somewhat later than Paul. But then verifying almost any rabbinic evidence from Paul's day is notoriously difficult. [36]

(3) The third possible background lies in Jewish apocalyptic. We have seen how the idea of "new heavens and a new earth" occurred in apocalyptic circles. The Intertestamental literature multiplied examples of the theme, and in certain writings (often difficult to date) we get references to the "Mighty One" coming to "renew his creation" (2 Baruch 32:6), the "new world" (2 Baruch 44:12), and "new creation" (Enoch 72:1). [37] If this background is accepted,

Paul would then here be saying that neither the uncircumcised state of Gentiles matters, nor the circumcision of Jews, but only the new apocalyptic creation which comes in Christ. But is this, then, a matter of the individual's conversion — new creaturehood — or does it imply (ontological) change for the whole cosmos — a new creation universally? On that score, unfortunately, the apocalyptic texts are open to interpretation, or manipulation, in both directions.

Several commentators have preferred this background in apocalyptic, and a recent article by Peter Stuhlmacher has employed it as a basis for further speculation.[38] Among the rabbis, he thinks, the cosmological aspect so prominent in some Intertestamental literature may have been receding and the anthropological application coming to the fore. In the face of early Christian use of the term in a cosmological sense, enthusiastically supposing the new age and new creation to be already fully here,[39] Stuhlmacher thinks Paul gave it a more ontic, realistic meaning, connected with baptism.

Of these three theories about backgrounds, my preference is for roots in Jewish proselyte baptism. No doubt, however, the phrase enjoyed apocalyptic associations in the minds of some. The exact nuance must be determined in the passages individually. One thing, however, that both verses share is a polemical thrust, against those who undervalue the new, or just possibly against apocalyptic over-enthusiasm.[40]

So far as form goes, commentators [41] have noted a structure in Galatians 6:15 which is similar to that at Galatians 5:6 and 1 Corinthians 7:19, a structure which runs "neither . . . , nor . . . , but . . . ."
1 Cor. 7:19, "*Neither* circumcision counts for anything, *nor* uncircumcision, *but* keeping the commandments of God."
(Presumably that is a formulation against those who ignore the ethical aspect of Christianity.)
Galatians 5:6, "In Christ Jesus *neither* circumcision *nor* uncircumcision is of any avail, *but* faith working through love."
(This is a more Pauline formulation of the same point.)
Galatians 6:15, "*Neither* circumcision *nor* uncircumcision means anything, *but kainē ktisis*."
Putting the three verses, so like in structure, together, one would

have an overall emphasis on new creation or creatures; faith working through love; and keeping the commandments of God as indicators of what Christianity involves.

In light of all this analysis, we may now ask what does Galatians 6:15 itself mean? In its context the verse speaks of the new in Christ, for which old physical conditions are no longer determinative (cf. Galatians 3:28). This new creation — and I prefer "new creaturehood" as a rendering — is linked to Christ's cross as the true expression of glory (6:14), and no doubt to baptism (3:27), which in Pauline thought is what actualizes the cross and new life from Christ.[42] The result is a new relationship and new outlook, a cruciform life-style (6:14) which applies not just for the isolated individual but corporately for the group "in Christ," the church, what 6:16 calls "the Israel of God." Those who sensed an ethical implication here are also correct; the "walk" or ethical conduct of the community is singled out in 6:16.

What is missing in the passage is any reference whatever to the cosmos or the world beyond believers or the nonhuman creation. The world, when it is mentioned, is the cosmos that stands in opposition to the cross (6:14). Hence the rendering "new creature" or creaturehood of the Christian believer is to be preferred.

2 Corinthians 5:17 depicts, in its context, the results of the work of God in Christ as justification and reconciliation with God and each other (5:21), but also as something like the first creation itself, only better (cf. 2 Corinthians 4:6). We have already opted for the translation "new creature," as in the RSV note. We can insert as subject and verb (missing in the Greek) either "he is" or "there is" a new creature; the former makes satisfactory sense (as the RSV has it). The punctuation option possible in the Greek, to read, "If someone is a new creature in Christ, the old has passed away, behold the new has come," is allowable, but does not seem to change the sense greatly. It may be noted that we have here, almost as an amplifying comment, a reflection of Deutero-Isaiah, 43:18, "the things of old remember not"; cf. also Isaiah 65:17.

The passage emphasizes that the man in Christ, who has experienced God's righteousness and the thrill of reconciliation, is a new creature. For him, the old is gone, "lo, new things have come," as the Greek says literally. But there is no talk here of an apocalyptically renovated cosmos (the grass is not any greener, the sunsets no more colorful than in pagan days). But there is a totally new relationship with God, with other men, and with self. Again, however, I would insist, the matter is not just one concerning the individual, as verse 17 by itself might suggest; it affects "us" (plural, vv. 18, 19, 20). But the world that God seeks to reconcile is here the world of men, those who believe and receive the reconciliation now accomplished, the reconciliation/justification/new creaturehood which comes from the death of Jesus (vv. 14, 15).

Stuhlmacher [43] has suggested a parallel here between Paul's own apostolic experience and status (mentioned in v. 16) and the situation of all Christians (v. 16, "any man" — and every man in Christ). The parallel is that calling and conversion leads to and shapes Christian existence. At 4:6 Paul uses creation language to describe his own case; in 5:17ff. he is using "new creaturehood" as a term to describe the experience of all Christians. Thus, the new creation reference here, as at Galatians 6:15, is really to new creatures, Christians. I do not find any apocalyptic vision of the cosmos renewed in these verses.

But there is one final question we must ask and answer if this interpretation of the new creation is to be sustained. What of Romans 8:18ff.? There, surely, the creation *(ktisis)* involves more than the totality of Christians. In Romans 8 not only the whole human creation but also the inanimate world as well, many commentators think, is groaning, waiting for the liberty the sons of God already have in Christ.

It will save a great deal of difficulty if we can recognize here an apocalyptic fragment in verses 19-22 imbedded in Paul's argument.[44] It is an apocalypse (the Greek term *apokalypsis* and its cognate verb are employed) about how the creation, subjected to futility (as in Genesis 3), waits to be set free from its bondage to decay. That kind of liberty the children of God already have (in Christ), while the rest of the world wails in birth pangs, waiting to be reborn. Such language unquestionably is apocalyptic in its hope and concepts.

But why does Paul quote such an apocalyptic patch? What is its function in the passage as a whole? Probably to correct certain Christian enthusiasts who think that, because they have the first fruits of the Spirit, they already have arrived in gloryland. Paul insists that glory-time is "not yet"; the believer must first pass through suffering (cf. 8:17, which sets the theme for 8:18ff.).

Thus Paul employs a passage from apocalyptic to address enthusiasts who deny suffering as a part of Christian life. But how does he interpret this apocalyptic quotation? Verses 23 and following give his application. In it there is not a word about the inanimate world of nature, or even of non-Christians. The whole concern is with believers, Christians, "we who have the first fruits, the Spirit" (v. 23). Contrary to what the enthusiasts suppose, we Christians (even the apostles, cf. 1 Corinthians 4:8-13) have not arrived as yet, our redemption is not complete. We still live in hope and not yet by sight. Hence the watchwords are "patience" (v. 25) and "prayer" in our weakness (vv. 26ff.).

The thrust of the passage is clear. Paul can and does cite words that look for a cosmic redemption. His interest in quoting them is entirely, however, on man, Christian man. The most recent analysis of Romans 8:19-22, by the German Catholic, Anton Vögtle,[45] concludes that the passage is not a "creation theology" but an expression of anthropology and soteriology.

Romans 8 thus fits with the interpretation we have reached of the new creation as the new creaturehood of Christian believers, not a cosmic day-dream.

V

Some Conclusions
about Creation
and New Creation

We have now traversed, selectively, many centuries and a variety of sources in the biblical witness: the Yahwist, some ten centuries before Christ; the sequence of prophets and psalmists in Israel; Deutero-Isaiah and his school, and the train of apocalyptists following in succeeding centuries; the note of newness in Jesus and the apostles' kerygma; the seldom-noted voice of pre-Pauline Christianity; Paul himself, and, more briefly, figures in the school of Paul and other New Testament writers; and the apocalyptic strand in early Christianity surfacing in the late first and even the second century A.D. (Revelation and 2 Peter). We have explored history-of-religion connections, asked the meaning of hymns, myths, and slogans quoted, and what the biblical writer intended with each. The initial creation, continuing creation, and new creatures in Christ, as well as any implications for the whole cosmos, have occupied our attention.

Can now any conclusions be drawn, especially in light of some of the broader questions posed above in Chapter I?

We begin with what seems the heart of the matter for biblical faith, new creation, in light of which experience statements are made about creation. *New creation* in the Bible refers to the converted believer, or, in the plural, the redeemed community. It is creation terminology used most powerfully to talk about redemption. *Kainē ktisis* thus turns out to be a "redemption term."

If the new creation involves, as Professor Sittler puts it, "a

100

promise, a faith, and a program," [1] we must now add that it is foremost a people – the people of God; for the New Testament, it is the people who are "in Christ." They are the spearhead of God's program and must for all practical purposes work it out as servants of the Lord.

But does *kainē ktisis* ever in the Bible refer to the world, to the entire cosmos, ontologically or in some way transformed? Not, we have found, in Galatians 6:15 or 2 Corinthians 5:17. In the apocalyptic passage quoted at Romans 8:19-22, yes, *ktisis* does refer to the world awaiting transformation, at least in the pre-Pauline form cited and the intent of it as apocalyptic. But though Paul uses this apocalyptic vision involving the entire universe in Romans 8, he himself does not go on in 8:23ff. to develop or discuss the non-human aspect, or even the situation of nonbelievers; he concentrates on those in Christ. The situation is similar in Revelation 21 and Isaiah 65-66. There the phrase "new heavens and new earth" sounds cosmological, but it is interpreted by the biblical writer in terms of the people of God and their new Jerusalem. Thus, there may have been moments of ecstasy when apocalyptists or enthusiasts talked of the whole universe from a vision of faith; but their rhetoric is consistently toned down as the Bible explicates the new heavens and earth, the new creation as the redeemed community.

As for *creation*, to sum up what we have found, the Bible's talk about creation:

1) always uses *language of the day*, including the world's terms and current scientific thought and theories – Babylonian, Stoic, or whatever – about how life began. The "how" comes from current science.

2) The Bible insists, in light of its experience with God and his salvation, that this God of the exoduses is the creator. But that is a *statement of faith*, spoken as creed or in hymnic form or, if as a narrative, in a mood of faith and doxologically of praise. The "who" of creation – namely, that it is God who created, "and Yahweh is his name," and Jesus Christ his son played a part – derives from redemption.

3) The Bible insists again and again that creation as God's work did not end when he made the earth and the fulness thereof, "in the beginning." God stands by, he sustains, he providentially inter-

venes, he gets involved. And so *creation continues*. But such a continuing creation is also an experience and testimony buttressed by faith.

4) This testimony of faith can project itself into *the future*. The God of creation, who brings the rain and sun, seedtime and harvest, the faithful Creator who "cares for you" (1 Peter 4:19; 5:7), will continue his providence, faith believes, and one day will carry out his promises. Creation thus reaches into the future, usually via apocalyptic language, and promises a new creation.

5) God's creative work, while involving the whole world, is especially understood in the Bible to affect men. At times "the world" equals nothing other than the world of men (cf. John 3:16-18!). Often the focus is specifically on Israel as the heart of God's creation, or, as with "new creation," on the New Israel or church. Thus, whether creation is thought of as initial creation at the beginning, continuing creation, or future creation, the formulations in the Bible have an *anthropological or existential thrust*. Man and his existence are the concern.

6) The *relation of creation and redemption* has been a major problem in modern theology, the connection of nature and history. In general we have found:

a) The formula which we have used before (where R denotes "redemption" and C "creation"), $\dfrac{R}{C}$, holds up; that is, redemption takes priority and dominates over creation. It is the redeemed community that speaks concerning creation. Creation/new creation language turns out usually to be in the service of the redemption motif.

b) On occasion, however, there can be creation material standing by itself — 1 Corinthians 8:6, with no mention of the cross; certain Psalm passages; Romans 8:19-22, with its apocalyptic hope; the uninterpreted phrase "new heavens and new earth." That would suggest "C" by itself. But examination of the context showed the redeemed community to be the confessor, the phrases usually to be interpreted anthropologically, and thrust to be "creative-redemptive."

c) A curious by-product of our investigation is the fact that creation itself often turns out to be understood as a type of redemption. If the original creation be depicted as a chaos-battle, then creation really is a redemptive triumph of Yahweh, defeating hostile forces; creation is his victory. If Stuhlmueller is at all correct, the heavy creation emphasis in Deutero-Isaiah is really in the service of redemption and a new exodus. Hence, "new creation" is a redemptive category too, that can best be expressed not by the symbol "C" alone but as "R" or better "C-R" (creative-redemption).

d) Part of our problem is semantic, in the way we define "creation" and "redemption." As working distinctions for biblical theology, one might propose the following for consideration:

creation is an action of God, reflecting his power and goodness, affecting all men and at times the world of nature;

redemption is an action of God, reflecting his power and goodness, affecting those in Israel or "in Christ" who accept his acts as salvation and new life.

On these definitions, those who experience R (redemption) often go on to talk of C (creation), in faith. In terms of a formula: R → C.

But are there any cases in the Bible of people who start with creation (C) and stop at that point, without having had the experience of redemption? or who, in light of C, go on to experience and speak of R? Logically we cannot deny the possibility, but in the biblical examples we have examined, the phenomenon does not seem to occur.[2]

John Gibbs [3] has sought to outflank the problem of the relation between creation and redemption with the formula:

$$\frac{\text{L (lordship of Christ)}}{\overbrace{\text{C (creation)} \qquad \text{R (redemption)}}}.$$

That equation works tolerably well in showing that it is the same God and same Lord who stand over both creation and redemption, and suggests two realms of divine activity. Certainly it holds good for those who experience redemption, confess the lordship, and then speak in faith of creation; in chart form:

But does it ever happen that someone who speaks of creation, apart from redemption, goes on to confess the lordship of his creator deity? i.e.,

In the Old Testament, with regard to God, possibly. Regarding Christ, I doubt it. Moreover, for the New Testament we have seen, the picture is that both God and Christ are involved in both creation and redemption.

Hence, perhaps the fairest formula we can put down is one that suggests the actual situation: the believer who has experienced redemption confesses the One who has delivered and made him what he is, through the action of creative redemption (C-R), which experience is then extrapolated back to the beginning of time, is confessed continually, and is hoped for in the time to come. In chart form:

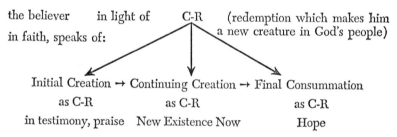

the believer   in light of   C-R   (redemption which makes him
in faith, speaks of: a new creature in God's people)

Initial Creation → Continuing Creation → Final Consummation
     as C-R   as C-R   as C-R
in testimony, praise   New Existence Now   Hope

If those who do *not* share in this redemption that the community knows or its hope or new existence now, nonetheless want to join in some part of this view of initial creation and of the world as God's, or of continuing providence, so much the better. It is questionable whether, without a fuller confession of Yahweh (or of Jesus), they can be rightly called "Israelites" ("Christians"), but they share at least this aspect of the faith.

Our final concern must, however, not be with those persons who may talk, along with us in the community of faith, of God as creator, without sharing the faith in God's redemptive work or in Christ as redeemer or agent of creation, but with those Christians who profess redemption but have not been enough concerned with the creation — with God's world and with their fellow men. Hence, a final point: 7) *the place of the Christian community in God's plan for the world.*

We have encountered this notion, that the community has such a role, in connection with 1 Corinthians 8:6. It took the form there of a claim that those who confess God and Christ as creator and redeemer may have a special role, living redemptively, to permeate "all things" until "the time when all things are 'for God.' " [4] We tentatively suggested the metaphors of "salt" and "light for the world" as describing the task of the Christian community (Matthew 5:13f.).[5] How shall this relation of Jesus' followers to the rest of men be understood? Among the options we note four.

One traditional solution has been to adopt the answer of apocalyptic: hang on and wait till God intervenes miraculously to convert all men and lead the pagans up to Jerusalem as believers. That task God himself will carry out supernaturally.[6] Much as this solution has biblical roots in certain prophetic-apocalyptic passages, is it, twenty centuries after the announcement of the parousia, still tenable today as *the* solution? (To reject it does not imply apocalyptic is valueless, however; only that Christians have no warrant to depend solely on a *deus ex machina* to carry out the Great Commission of Matthew 28:19-20 or to "cop out" on responsibility in the world.) This first counsel amounts to saying "Wait for God," and nothing more.

A second answer, modern in its tone but building on what we have just said, is to allow that the dream of the conversion of the world is just a dream — that, indeed, the language of faith is Christian rhetoric, and that all religions are after all pretty much the same. The net effect of this approach is to eschew all efforts to permeate the rest of the world with the lordship of Christ. It is to forswear mission. Christians may, it is said, believe what they will, but let others do the same. What this view rightly sees is that there are other faiths and other experiences which make their confessions too. The solution advocated here is tolerance of other religions, but little more. The result would be a tolerant status quo in the world of "many gods and many lords" (save for aggressive religions which do not accept such counsel). Since the age of reason and its plea for religious tolerance, many Christians have in effect adopted this attitude of "live and let live." The second solution thus amounts to passive tolerance.

A third solution is more recent: to declare in effect all men to be "Christic," to be "anonymously Christian," even if they do not know it.[7] Here "grace" is identified as common to both R and C, and whoever partakes of the good or does good in any way is reckoned to be within the sphere of the cosmic Christ and the new creation.

Quite apart from a certain christological megalomania implied and possible violation of honest pagans in thus claiming them for Christ against their will or secretly, this view misses the nature of the new creation as a redemptive term, and confuses the case of human goodness or man's admission of C as God's work, with the specific and full acknowledgment of C-R as the work of God-in-Christ. In spite of these seeming confusions, it is a powerfully attractive option today, and does catch up the Bible's most universal hopes. Small wonder that this solution, which amounts to saying "Grace may be assumed to be always already there and is the work of Christ," has had appeal in a land like India. But even so, it, too, is a statement of faith — which the Bible does not seem to make.

The fourth solution is that expressed by the author of Colossians and the rest, I believe, of the New Testament. Colossians 1:15-20 confesses that Christ who reconciled us by his blood and who is the first born from the dead (1:20, 18) is also the first born of all creation, through whom all things were made (1:15-16). This message of C-R is to be spread throughout the entire world (*ta panta*), but it is to happen through the preaching of the word (1:23, 25, 28), by the body of Christ, the church (1:18, 24f.). The means is, as Eduard Schweizer puts it, the missionary body of Christ, i.e., you and I.[8] Any cosmic permeation with the message of Christ as C-R is the task of the community that confesses him as creator-lord and redeemer-lord. The fourth answer thus is "mission."

This last solution, which in my opinion conforms to the Bible's view of creative-redemption, runs every danger, of course, of leading to Christian arrogance, intolerance, and, when the task proves too tough, dismay and lethargy. Surely all these results have happened in the past. But it is the presence of the church's Lord, as C-R continues, that counters the factors of lethargy and dismay. Against arrogance and intolerance, which are real menaces, the saving graces are (a) the call for a servant image in God's people, characteristic of Deutero-Isaiah's dreams and of the New Testament; (b) an awareness that God can use other means to achieve his purposes than the church community (e.g., Cyrus as messiah in Isaiah 44:28; 45:1ff.), especially if the church falls into despondence or self-pity; and (c) the fact we have acknowledged, that there are others who revere the created world and a creator even if they have not given Jesus Christ full place such as he has in the New Testament. This qualification should keep Christians from pride and arrogance as they labor for the lord, but with all men of good will in God's world.

All this calls for a Christian strategy of keeping up the church's confession and praise of God, continuing its mission and witness in hope, and cooperating fully with all those who share a passion for God's world, if not always for his word.

The last category mentioned in this strategy comes especially into play in matters of social concern in a pluralistic society, such as America or India. The Christian as new creature has a momentum and understands the "why" of concern for others. But the "how" for action will be dictated by circumstances, in cooperation with people of other persuasions of faith who share in his view of creation or who share with him fellow creaturehood and common humanity.

Likewise with what we called the stewardship of creation.[9] The believer's understanding of redemption will impel him into the world of God's creation with a special passion for its wise use and care. But he will meet with others who, while not sharing his view of redemption, do have this passion too, perhaps as great as his, or even greater, for the earth. With them he is to work, in completely good conscience.

Left hanging till the end, as always, is the question of apocalyptic. This the believer can not always take literally, but the element of hope which its language gives, and the trust beyond ourselves to One outside our daily realm are values always needed for life now which must be preserved.

New creatures, then, speaking of creation with some of the richness and variety which the Bible offers — these are twin emphases the church today needs.

Creation! It belongs to God, but is entrusted to all of us, as mankind, who are the creatures and climax of God's creation.

But especially is the creation a gift and challenge for those who name the name of Christ, the new creatures of God. For them old things readily pass away, there is a vision of the new to be. All things, Paul insists, writing to just such believers, are yours, for you belong to Christ, and Christ is God's. To whom be glory, praise, and dominion now and ever more.

And we cannot help but add, as Paul would, even at his most exalted theological moments (cf. 1 Corinthians 15-16:1): To work, as good stewards! And look redeemed!

Notes

I: NEW INTEREST IN CREATION AND NEW CREATION

1. In *The Human Crisis in Ecology,* ed. by Franklin L. Jensen and Cedric W. Tilberg (New York: Lutheran Church in America, Board of Social Ministry, 1972), pp. 101f. (Chapter Six is the work primarily of Professor Sittler.)

2. *Creation: The Impact of an Idea,* ed. by Daniel O'Connor and Francis Oakley (Scribner Source Books in Religion; New York: Charles Scribner's Sons, 1969), pp. 2, 4.

3. Cf. H. Paul Santmire, *Brother Earth* (New York: Thomas Nelson, 1970). "Sister nature" was popularized by Joseph A. Sittler Jr., in "Called to Unity," *The Ecumenical Review* 14 (1961-62): 177-187.

4. Translation from the International Consultation on English Texts, in *Prayers we have in common* (Philadelphia: Fortress, 1970), pp. 9, 11.

5. E.g., Langdon Gilkey, *Maker of Heaven and Earth: A Study of the Christian Doctrine of Creation* (New York: Doubleday, 1959; Anchor Books ed., 1965).

6. *The Essence of Christianity,* trans. by George Eliot (reprinted, New York: Harper & Row, 1957), p. 287.

7. *The Flight from Creation* (Minneapolis: Augsburg, 1971). A critical appraisal is given by H. Paul Santmire, "Wingren's hope-less theology: 'backward tunnel vision,'" in *Lutheran Forum* 5, 9 (November, 1971): 24, 26; and in *Interpretation* 26 (1972): 368-372.

8. T. S. Eliot, "Choruses from 'The Rock,'" III, lines 35-36.

9. "Stewardship" is stressed in *The Human Crisis in Ecology* (cited above, note 1), pp. 76f., but its meaning as based on creation (Article One) rather than on redemption (Article Two) remains to be worked out.

God's Stewards: A Theological Study of the Principles and Practices of Stewardship, by Helge Brattgård, trans. by Gene J. Lund (Minneapolis: Augsburg, 1963), is clearly christocentric in perspective. Could a similar study be worked out based on creation?

10. I have dealt with the concept of *oikonomia* in an unpublished Ph.D. dissertation and series of subsequent articles, and am convinced the use of the phrase *oikos theou*, employed in *The Human Crisis in Ecology* (cited above, note 1), p. 22, points to a rich background in this Stoic (and also Semitic and early Christian) concept.

11. Carl E. Braaten, *Christ and Counter-Christ: Apocalyptic Themes in Theology and Culture* (Philadelphia: Fortress, 1972), p. 119.

12. *Crisis in Eden: A Religious Study of Man and Environment* (New York: Abingdon, 1970).

13. O'Connor and Oakley, *Creation* (cited above, note 2), p. 1.

14. *On the Prescription against Heretics*, 7.

15. "Creation and Environment," *The Expository Times* 83 (1971-72): 4-9.

16. Harvey Cox, *The Secular City* (New York: Macmillan, 1965), cf. pp. 22f. Johannes Metz, *Theology of the World* (New York: Herder & Herder, 1969), cf. pp. 65f.

17. Lynn White Jr., "The Historical Roots of Our Ecologic Crisis," *Science* 155 (1967): 1203-1207; reprinted in *The Environmental Handbook*, ed. by Garrett de Bell (New York: Ballentine, 1970), pp. 12-26, and elsewhere. White's position is criticized as oversimply blaming Judeo-Christian teaching for the ecological crisis by Lewis W. Moncrief, "The Cultural Basis for Our Environmental Crisis," *Science* 170 (1970): 511; and by Richard T. Wright, "Responsibility for the Ecological Crisis," *Bioscience* August 1, 1970, p. 852, quoted in *The Human Crisis in Ecology* (cited above, note 1), p. xv. Cf. James Barr, "Man and Nature — The Ecological Controversy and the Old Testament," *Bulletin of the John Rylands Library* (Manchester) 55 (1972): 9-32, who is doubtful that the Judeo-Christian doctrine of creation has either caused scientific progress or led to nature's thralldom.

18. *Marxism and Radical Revolution*, ed. by John C. Raines and Thomas Dean (Philadelphia: Temple University Press, 1970), p. 7.

19. "Creation and Environment" (cited above, note 15), p. 5.

20. *Ibid.*

21. Lynn White (cited above, note 17), p. 1207.

22. Paul E. Lutz, in *The Human Crisis in Ecology* (cited above, note 1), p. xiii.

23. Cf. Bultmann's *Theology of the New Testament*, trans. by Kendrick Grobel, 2 vols. (New York: Scribner's, 1951, 1955), Vol. 1, pp. 329f., 348; *Faith and Understanding I*, ed. by R. W. Funk, trans. by Louise Pettibone Smith (New York: Harper & Row, 1969), pp. 202f., 233, and passim.

24. *The New Being* (New York: Scribner's, 1955): "If I were asked to sum up the Christian message for our time in two words, I would say with Paul: It is the message of a 'New Creation'" (p. 15).

25. Cf. *All Things New* (Preparatory Booklet for the Fourth Assembly of the World Council of Churches, Uppsala, Sweden, July 4-20, 1968) and other literature from the meeting. Important as background is the study "God in Nature and History," in *New Directions in Faith and Order, Bristol 1967* (Geneva: World Council of Churches, Faith and Order Paper No. 50, 1968), pp. 7-31.

26. E.g., *Apocalypticism*, ed. R. W. Funk (Journal for Theology and the Church, 6; New York: Herder & Herder, 1969); cf. the various writings of Pannenberg and others in Germany and Carl Braaten and others in the United States.

27. Braaten, *Christ and Counter-Culture* (cited above, note 11), presents chapters back-to-back on "Apocalyptic Theology of Revolution," and "Toward an Ecological Theology" (pp. 101-134). When the "Spirituality of Hope" (pp. 82-100) and "Eschatology and the Future of Religions" (pp. 135-48) are added, one has a concatenation of themes which adhere in modern discussion to the idea of "new creation."

28. *The Human Crisis in Ecology* (cited above, note 1), p. 99.

29. The terminology is suggested by John G. Gibbs, *Creation and Redemption: A Study in Pauline Theology* (Leiden: Brill, 1971). Cf. also his article, "Pauline Cosmic Christology and the Ecological Crisis," *Journal of Biblical Literature* 90 (1971): 466-479.

30. *The Human Crisis in Ecology* (cited above, note 1), p. 90.

II: FAITH SPEAKS ABOUT CREATION

1. So O'Connor and Oakley, *Creation* (cited above, Chap. I, note 2), p. 4.

2. The full hymn texts are found in the Lutheran *Service Book and Hymnal* (1958), numbers 414, verse 1; 205, verses 1 and 2; and 62, verse 1; and for the text by Daniel Thambyrajah Niles, from the Tamil original, in the *E.A.C.C. Hymnal* (Tokyo, published by the East Asia Christian Conference, 1963), number 191, verse 1 and refrain.

3. On the theology of Zion and the temple at Jerusalem, cf. Bernhard W. Anderson, *Creation Versus Chaos: The Reinterpretation of Mythical Symbolism in the Bible* (New York: Association Press, 1967), pp. 64-68, 76f., 102, 107, 113; Gerhard von Rad, *Old Testament Theology*, trans. by D. M. G. Stalker, 2 vols. (New York: Harper & Row, 1962, 1965), Vol. 1, pp. 46-48; Roland de Vaux, O.P., *Ancient Israel: Its Life and Institutions*, trans. by John McHugh (New York: McGraw-Hill, 1961), pp. 325-330.

4. On the history of the doctrine of creation in Christian thought, see Gilkey, *Maker of Heaven and Earth* (cited above, Chap. I, note 5).

5. A book emphasizing this variety has even appeared under the title *New Testament Disunity: Its Significance for Christianity Today*, by John Charlot (New York: E. P. Dutton, 1970).

6. Cf. S. G. F. Brandon, *Creation Legends of the Ancient Near East* (London: Hodder & Stoughton, 1963; Mystic, Conn.: Lawrence Verry, Inc.). More briefly, the chapter entitled "In the Beginning" in Brandon's *Religion in Ancient History: Studies in Ideas, Men and Events* (New York: Scribner's, 1969), pp. 18-30. Further, S. N. Kramer (ed.), *Mythologies of the Ancient World* (Garden City, N.Y.: Doubleday, Anchor Books, 1961). The documents themselves are accessible in translation in the definitive collection edited by James B. Pritchard, *Ancient Near Eastern Texts Relating to the Old Testament* (Princeton: University Press, 2d ed., 1955; cited below from the 3d ed. with Supplement, 1969).

7. For background, consult the standard commentaries, e.g., C. K. Barrett, *A Commentary on the First Epistle to the Corinthians* (Harper's/Black's New Testament Commentaries series, London: A. & C. Black, New York: Harper & Row, 1968), or treatments in one-volume Bible commentaries. The discussion which follows owes much, of course, to recent and past specialized literature, such as is listed in Hans Conzelmann's volume on this epistle in the Meyer Kritisch-Exegetischer Kommentar, *Der erste Brief an die Korinther* (Göttingen: Vandenhoeck & Ruprecht, 11. Auflage, 1969).

8. On the use here of *Kyrios* for Jesus, see Werner Kramer, *Christ, Lord, Son of God*, trans. by Brian Hardy (Studies in Biblical Theology, 50; London: SCM, and Naperville, Illinois: Allenson, 1966), pp. 94-99 and 222.

9. Eduard Lohse, "Zu I Cor. 10, 26, 31," *Zeitschrift für die neutestamentliche Wissenschaft* 47 (1956): 277-280.

10. The term is used by J. N. D. Kelly, *Early Christian Creeds* (London: Longmans, Green, & Company, 1950, 2d ed. 1960), pp. 19-22, to describe such credos with two articles.

11. The phrase is so employed by the Jewish historian Josephus who is contemporary with the later New Testament period, *Antiquities* 4.201, cf. 8.355, 5.112; *Against Apion* 2. 193 ("one temple for one God"), and was investigated by Erik Peterson, *Heis Theos: Epigraphische, formgeschichtliche und religionsgeschichtliche Untersuchungen* (Forschungen zur Literatur des Alten und Neuen Testaments, 41; Göttingen: Vandenhoeck & Ruprecht, 1926). Material is conveniently summarized by Vernon H. Neufeld, *The Earliest Christian Confessions* (New Testament Tools and Studies, 5; Grand Rapids: Eerdmans, Leiden: Brill, 1963), pp. 34-41.

12. Cf. Eduard Norden, *Agnostos Theos: Untersuchungen zur Form-*

geschichte Religiöser Rede (Leipzig: Teubner, 1913, 4th ed. reprinted Stuttgart: Teubner, 1956).

13. Marcus Aurelius, *Meditations* 4.23.

14. Cf. Kramer, *Christ, Lord, Son of God* (cited above, note 8), pp. 65f., 158f., 167f.; and Neufeld, *Earliest Christian Confessions* (cited above, note 11), pp. 56ff.

15. So Hans Conzelmann, *An Outline of the Theology of the New Testament,* trans. by John Bowden (New York: Harper & Row, 1969), p. 171.

16. *Ibid.,* p. 202.

17. Cf. Robert M. Grant, "Causation and 'the Ancient World View,'" *Journal of Biblical Literature* 83 (1964): 34-40. There is an even more complicated use of prepositions in Philo's essay "On the Cherubim," sections 125-127.

18. *Service Book and Hymnal* 596, verse 4.

19. Cf. Gibbs, *Creation and Redemption* (cited above, Chap. I, note 29), pp. 59-73 who treats these verses as one of six key passages in the Pauline corpus. In general, however, Gibbs's study does not discriminate sharply enough among pre-Pauline materials, genuine Pauline redaction, and deutero-Pauline documents, though the book improves in this respect on his earlier doctoral dissertation upon which it is based. Cf. the reviews by Robert J. Karris, O.F.M., in the *Catholic Biblical Quarterly* 34 (1972): 218-220; and by Ralph P. Martin in the *Journal of Biblical Literature* 91 (1972): 429-431.

20. As is claimed by Robert M. Grant, in *The Early Christian Doctrine of God* (Charlottesville, Virginia: University Press of Virginia, 1966), p. 6.

21. Gibbs, *Creation and Redemption* (cited above, Chap. I, note 29), p. 61.

22. A general picture of the Yahwist and his work is given by most surveys of the Old Testament, and an appreciation of his achievements and its relevance especially in the writings of von Rad, noted below, and in the book by Peter Ellis, C.SS.R., *The Yahwist: The Bible's First Theologian* (Notre Dame, Indiana: Fides Publishers, 1969; London: Geoffrey Chapman, 1969). See also H. W. Wolff, "The Kerygma of the Yahwist," *Interpretation* 20 (1966): 131-158.

23. Philadelphia: Fortress Press, 1971.

24. Jacob, *Das erste Buch der Tora, Genesis* (Berlin, 1934), as cited in Gerhard von Rad, *Genesis: A Commentary,* trans. by John M. Marks (The Old Testament Library, Philadelphia: Westminster, 1961), p. 75.

25. *The Old Testament: An Introduction,* trans. by Peter R. Ackroyd (New York: Harper & Row, 1965), pp. 194-204.

26. Cf. Brandon, *Creation Legends* (cited above, note 6), pp. 14-65. The other works listed in note 6 above also include some of this material.

27. *Ibid.,* pp. 66-90.

28. *Ibid.*, pp. 91-117.

29. Cf. A. Kapelrud, "Ugarit," in *The Interpreter's Dictionary of the Bible*, ed. by G. A. Buttrick (Nashville & New York: Abingdon, 1962), vol. 4, pp. 724-732; or Cyrus Gordon's treatment in S. Kramer, *Mythologies* (cited above, note 6), pp. 181-218.

30. Cf. von Rad, *Genesis* (cited above, note 24), p. 175. Also, Norman C. Habel, " 'Yahweh, Maker of Heaven and Earth': A Study in Tradition Criticism," *Journal of Biblical Literature* 91 (1972): 321-337.

31. For the text of the Egyptian hymn, see *Ancient Near Eastern Texts* (cited above, note 6), pp. 369-371; cf. the discussion of Psalm 104 by Lawrence Toombs in *The Interpreter's One-Volume Commentary on the Bible* (Nashville & New York: Abingdon, 1971).

32. *Genesis* (cited above, note 24), pp. 97f.; cf. also pp. 27-30, and further, von Rad's essay, "The Theological Problem of the Old Testament Doctrine of Creation" (1936), in his collected essays, *The Problem of the Hexateuch and Other Essays*, trans. by E. W. Trueman Dicken (New York: McGraw-Hill, and Edinburgh: Oliver & Boyd, 1966), pp. 131-143.

33. *Ibid., Genesis*, p. 98.

34. It is the author of 4 Ezra (II Esdras in the RSV Apocrypha), writing late in the first century A.D. after the fall of Jerusalem, who especially takes up the problem of sin in all its gravity, though some of the Qumran writings likewise reflect a similar view of man's predicament.

35. So von Rad, *Genesis* (cited above, note 24), pp. 77f., and many other commentators.

36. For the Adapa story, see *Ancient Near Eastern Texts* (cited above, note 6), pp. 101-103.

37. So E. A. Speiser, *Genesis* (Anchor Bible, 1; Garden City; Doubleday, 1964), pp. 20, 26f.

38. E.g., Cuthbert A. Simpson's exegetical treatment of Genesis in *The Interpreter's Bible* (Nashville & New York: Abingdon, 1952), pp. 441ff.

39. *Genesis* (cited above, note 24), p. 73.

40. The theory of a New Year's festival at the Jerusalem temple, akin to the Babylonian celebration with its myth and ritual, has especially been championed by Scandinavian scholars like Sigmund Mowinckel; see his book, *The Psalms in Israel's Worship*, trans. by D. R. Ap-Thomas, 2 vols. (Nashville & New York: Abingdon, 1962), in particular pp. 106-192. For brief discussion of the problem, cf. Anderson, *Creation Versus Chaos* (cited above, note 3); pp. 65, 83, 101f., 113f., etc.; further, H. H. Rowley, *Worship in Ancient Israel: Its Form and Meaning* (Philadelphia: Fortress, 1967), pp. 184ff.

41. Cf. R. W. Corney, "Zadok," *Interpreter's Dictionary of the Bible* (cited above, note 29), Vol. 4, pp. 928f.; and C. E. Hauer Jr., "Who Was Zadok?" *Journal of Biblical Literature* 82 (1963): 89-94.

42. See the references cited above in note 3. Space does not permit further exploration here of this strand of Old Testament theology so significant for creation as a theme.

43. The phrase is von Rad's; cf. his *Genesis* (cited above, note 24), pp. 27-30, and "The Theological Problem of . . . Creation" (cited above, note 32), pp. 68ff.

44. Especially in his works cited in notes 32 and 24 above.

45. *The Theology of the Book of Ruth* (Facet Books, Biblical Series, 24; Philadelphia: Fortress, 1969).

46. So Rowley, *Worship in Ancient Israel* (cited above, note 40), p. 87.

47. That Nathan was the Yahwist is the solution of Emmanuel Lewy, *The Growth of the Pentateuch* (New York: Bookman Associates, 1955), pp. 186ff.; cf. Ellis, *The Yahwist* (cited above, note 22), p. 21.

48. Cf. Ellis, *ibid.*

49. Cited above, note 22.

50. On Genesis 1, see von Rad's commentary, *Genesis* (cited above, note 24), and his essay, "The Theological Problem of . . . Creation" (cited above, note 32); Claus Westermann, *The Genesis Accounts of Creation* (Facet Books, Biblical Series, 7; Philadelphia: Fortress, 1964), with further literature of a popular nature cited there; and, more technical, W. H. Schmidt, *Die Schöpfungsgeschichte der Priesterschrift: Zur Überlieferungsgeschichte von Genesis 1, 1–2, 4a* (Wissenschaftliche Monographien zum Alten und Neuen Testament, 17; Neukirchen-Vluyn: Neukirchener Verlag, 1964). On Colossians 1:15-20, see the discussion and literature cited below in the Excursus, pp. 42-56 (footnotes 52ff. below).

51. See Westermann's *Genesis Accounts* (cited above, note 50), and his book *The Praise of God in the Psalms*, trans. by Keith R. Crim (Richmond: John Knox Press, 1965).

52. Cf. *Christ and Humanity*, ed. by Ivar Asheim (Philadelphia: Fortress, 1970), pp. 96-109. A summary is given there of recent views in critical scholarly literature, especially that in German, by Gabathuler, Kehl, Eduard Schweizer, Käsemann, J. M. Robinson, Deichgräber, and others, which has not been repeated below.

53. See especially the essay by Roy A. Harrisville, "The New Testament Witness to the Cosmic Christ," in *The Gospel and Human Destiny* (Minneapolis: Augsburg, 1971), pp. 39-63. The German commentary by Eduard Lohse (then Professor of New Testament at Göttingen, now Bishop of Hannover, succeeding Hanns Lilje) in the Meyer series has recently been translated into English by R. Poehlmann and R. J. Karris, *Colossians and Philemon* (Hermeneia series; Philadelphia: Fortress, 1971); see pp. 41-61. The treatment by Gibbs in *Creation and Redemption* (cited above, Chap. 1, note 29) fails to recognize clearly the import of a source and the editing of it by the author of the epistle. For a some-

what different analysis, cf. Bruce Vawter, "The Colossian Hymn and the Principle of Redaction," *Catholic Biblical Quarterly* 33 (1971): 62-81.

54. Thus, for example the treatment by C. F. D. Moule, *The Epistles of Paul the Apostle to the Colossians and to Philemon* (Cambridge Greek Testament; New York: Cambridge University Press, 1957), pp. 60-62, rightly rejects the theory that we deal with insertions later interpolated into Colossians by the author of Ephesians, but does not deal with the view that the author himself of Colossians may be employing a source.

55. Minor adjustments have been made in wording, e.g., translation of the opening participle in v. 12 as an imperative, and preference for the reading "you" in v. 12 as in the RSV note; on such details, cf. Lohse's commentary (cited above, note 53). Readers will note that the following phrases in the RSV are omitted above, for the time being; they will be explained below as later additions to the original hymn, most likely by the author of Colossians (rather than by an earlier hand):

v. 18*a*, "the church";
v. 20*c*, "by the blood of his cross."

56. Some of the varying opinions on the extent of the hymn and its exact arrangement are presented in *Christ and Humanity* (cited above, note 52). The version given above follows that accepted by Lohse, *Colossians* (cited above, note 53), pp. 44f., which differs from my earlier reconstruction in that it retains as part of the hymn vv. 16*cd* ("visible and invisible" plus the list of four elements in the heavenly hierarchy of powers); 18*d* ("that in everything he might be preeminent"); and 20*b* ("making peace through him"). I should agree with Lohse that the two items treated as interpretative additions in note 55 above and in our discussion below are far more likely of demonstration as insertions than are the three just listed. Involved is the question of whether we think the two stanzas of the hymn were originally exactly parallel to each other or only relatively so.

57. Moule, *Colossians* (cited above, note 54), pp. 13f., defends Pauline authorship; Lohse, *Colossians* (cited above, note 53), pp. 4, 181, concludes that "a theologian schooled in Pauline thought composed the letter."

58. All commentators from Lightfoot on (who as early as the 1870s proposed connections between the thought of the opponents in Colossae and the Essenes) have dealt with the question; cf. Moule, *Colossians* (cited above, note 54), pp. 29-34, and Lohse, *Colossians* (cited above, note 53), pp. 127-131.

59. See the treatment by Jack T. Sanders, *The New Testament Christological Hymns: Their Historical Religious Background* (Society of New Testament Studies Monograph Series, 15; New York: Cambridge University Press, 1971), pp. 12-14 and 75-87.

60. See above, pp. 28f

61. See Eduard Schweizer's article on "body," *sōma*, in the *Theological*

Dictionary of the New Testament, ed. by G. Kittel and G. Friedrich (Grand Rapids: Eerdmans), Vol. 7 (1971), pp. 1024-1091, especially pp. 1029f., 1032, and 1074-1076; and Lohse, *Colossians* (cited above, note 53), pp. 42f., 53.

62. Cf. Sanders, *Christological Hymns* (cited above, note 59), where further references are cited and views summarized on each passage.

63. London: Nisbet & Co.

64. *Ibid.*, p. vii.

65. *Ibid.*, p. 55.

66. "Called to Unity" (cited above, Chap. I, note 3).

67. Cf. Lohse, *Colossians* (cited above, note 53), 41ff.; and *Christ and Humanity* (cited above, note 52), pp. 96ff.

68. In addition to the discussions cited in note 67, see especially the treatments by Eduard Schweizer: *"sōma"* (cited above, note 61); *The Church as the Body of Christ* (Chime Books; Richmond: John Knox Press, 1964); and "The Church as the Missionary Body of Christ," originally in *New Testament Studies* 8 (1961-62): 1-11, reprinted in Schweizer's *Neotestamentica: Deutsche und Englische Aufsätze 1951-1963* (Zurich: Zwingli Verlag, 1963), pp. 317-329.

69. *Evangelisch-Katholischer Kommentar zum Neuen Testament, Vorarbeiten Heft 1* (Zurich: Benziger Verlag, and Neukirchen-Vluyn: Neukirchener Verlag, 1969), pp. 97-103, summarized in *Christ and Humanity* (cited above, note 52), pp. 107-109.

70. Some of the literature is cited by Lohse, *Colossians* (cited above, note 53), pp. 60f., note 211. It is only fair to add that even in World Council circles there has been criticism of "cosmic Christology"; cf. H. H. Wolf, "Christ at Work in History: In the light of the 'Barmen Declaration of 1934' of the confessing Church of Germany," *The Ecumenical Review* 18 (1966): 1-20, with a response by M. M. Thomas, pp. 21-26. Wolf is critical of the tendency to find "Christ at work among mankind apart from and outside the actual preaching of the Gospel," especially, as M. M. Thomas had implied, in revolutionary political movements of Asia and Africa. At issue is not the claim that God the Creator and Sustainer is at work in the world, but that God the Redeemer and Reconciler, Jesus Christ, is bringing about the new creation by such political and often violent means.

71. I am grateful to the Reverends D. J. C. Duraisingh and A. P. Nirmal, of United Theological College, Bangalore, for suggestions they shared in this area. For titles to 1965, cf. Kaj Baago, *A Bibliography* (Library of Indian Christian Theology; Madras: Christian Literature Society, for United Theological College, Bangalore, 1969). Among the significant treatments are Choan-Seng Song, "The Witness to Christ in the World of Religions and Cultures," *The South East Asia Journal of Theology* 2, 3 (January, 1961): 20-25, and "The Role of Christology in the Christian Encounter with Eastern Religions," *ibid.*, 5, 3 (January,

1964): 13-31; the June, 1962 issue of *Religion and Society* (Bangalore; Vol. 9, No. 2), devoted to "Doctrines of Creation" (but chiefly with regard to Hindu thought); R. V. De Smet and Paul Hacker, "Materials for an Indian Christology," *Religion and Society* 12,4 (December, 1965): 6-15; *The Indian Journal of Theology*, 15, 3 and 4 (1966), on "The Cosmic Christ" (see below, note 72); and the issue of *Religion and Society* for September, 1964 (11,3), on "Indian Understandings of Jesus Christ." By and large, the concern in these articles is not, however, with Colossians 1 and the specific issues of "cosmic Christology" raised at New Delhi.

72. Because of their inaccessibleness to many in the West, I list the full titles for the articles in 15, 3 (July–September, 1966): J. C. Hindley, "The Christ of Creation in New Testament Theology," pp. 89-105; J. Dupuis, "The Cosmic Christ in the Early Fathers," 106-120; A. F. Thompson, "The Colossian Vision in Theology and Philosophy," 121-129; A. Bruggemann, S. J., "The Cosmic Christ: Some Recent Interpretations," 130-142; and 15, 4 (October–December, 1966): J. Bayart, S. J., "The Cosmic Christ and Other Religions," 145-149; and P. Fallon, S.J., "The Cosmic Christ and the Asian Revolution," 150-153.

73. *Ibid.*, 15, 3 (1966): 96.

74. See Kaj Baago, *Pioneers of Indigenous Christianity* (Confessing the Faith in India Series, 4; Bangalore: Christian Institute for the Study of Religion and Society, and Madras: Christian Literature Society, 1969), pp. 1ff.; the phrases noted above are documented there on pp. 9, 12f., 3, and 17. The most extreme views, those of Parani Andi, reflect Free Masonry more than Christianity. For the general picture of development, cf. R. H. S. Boyd, "Indian Christian Thinking in Relation to Christ," *Religion and Society* 11, 3 (September, 1964): 61-71.

75. Comparison with Teilhard is made by Robin H. S. Boyd, *An Introduction to Indian Christian Theology* (Madras: Christian Literature Society, 1969), p. 32; on Sen, see Boyd's book, pp. 26-39, and M. M. Thomas, *The Acknowledged Christ of the Indian Renaissance* (Indian Theological Library, 4; Madras: Christian Literature Society, for the Senate of Serampore College, 1970), pp. 58-84. The oft-quoted statement, "The problem of creation was not how to produce one Christ, but how to make every man Christ," occurs in *Keshub Chunder* [sic] *Sen's Lectures in India* (The Brahma Samaj; London: Cassell, 1901), Lecture II, *That Marvellous Mystery — The Trinity* (1882), p. 15. Further, P. J. Santram, "Christ of the Brahmo Samaj Movement," *Religion and Society* 11, 3 (September, 1964): 7-12. There are interesting comments on Sen in Geoffrey Moorhouse, *Calcutta* (London: Weidenfeld & Nicolson, 1971), pp. 182f., 195, and 221; cf. 57f., 189, and 190 on the Brahma Samaj.

76. Thomas, *Acknowledged Christ* (cited above, note 75), p. 70. On "The hidden Christ," see Boyd, *Indian . . . Theology* (cited above, note 75), pp. 37-39. The statement quoted from Sen, which begins "Christ

is already present in you . . . ," is found in his *Lectures* (cited above, note 75), I, p. 391.

77. Thomas, *Acknowledged Christ* (cited above, note 75), p. 80.

78. On Brahmabandhab, cf. Boyd, *Indian . . . Theology* (cited above, note 75), pp. 58-85; Thomas, *Acknowledged Christ* (cited above, note 75), pp. 103-114; and Baago, *Pioneers* (cited above, note 74), pp. 26-49 and 118-150 (excerpts from his writings).

79. The comparison is made by Frederich Heiler, as cited in Thomas, *Acknowledged Christ* (cited above, note 75), p. 113; cf. Heiler's *The Gospel of Sadhu Sundar Singh*, abridged trans. by Olive Wyon (London: Allen & Unwin, 1927), pp. 219f. (reprint, Lucknow: Lucknow Publishing House, 1970, pp. 214f.).

80. See, e.g., the excerpt from Brahmabandhab's magazine *Sophia* for January, 1895, given in Baago, *Pioneers* (cited above, note 74), pp. 120-123.

81. There is a chapter devoted to him in Boyd, *Indian . . . Theology* (cited above, note 75), pp. 144-164. Further, D. A. Thangasamy, *The Theology of Chenchiah*, a collection of his writings (Confessing the Faith in India Series 1, 1967), and Thangasamy's article, "Chenchiah's Understanding of Jesus Christ," *Religion and Society* 11, 3 (September, 1964): 72-90. Additional literature is given in the footnotes of the books mentioned. Chenchiah was involved in the Madras group which published *Rethinking Christianity in India* (Madras: A. N. Sudarisanam, 1938), just prior to the world conference at Madras of the International Missionary Council in 1938. Chenchiah wrote five sections of that book, including "Jesus and Non-Christian Faiths," pp. 47-62. There is a brief reference to Chenchiah in Thomas, *Acknowledged Christ* (cited above, note 75), pp. 167-170 (on his opposition to Hendrik Kraemer's Barthian views), 322f., and passim. A chapter from a Serampore dissertation on him by S. Wesley Ariarajah is printed under the title "Chenchiah's Christology," in the *Bangalore Theological Forum*, 2, 1 (January, 1968): 47-61.

82. *Rethinking Christianity* (cited above, note 81), p. 62; and *National Christian Council Review* (Mysore), New Series 20 (1943), p. 363, as quoted in Boyd, *Indian . . . Theology* (cited above, note 75), pp. 149f.

83. *Indian . . . Theology* (cited above, note 75), pp. 144ff., especially 145.

84. *Ibid.*, pp. 150, 163, citing *Rethinking Christianity* (cited above, note 81), p. 187.

85. Cf. Boyd, *Indian . . . Theology* (cited above, note 75), pp. 186-205, especially 190-192. Devanandan's New Delhi address, "Called to Witness" (cf. Sittler's "Called to Unity," cited above, Chap. I, note 3), is printed in Devanandan's *Preparation for Dialogue: A Collection of Essays on Hinduism and Christianity in New India* (Bangalore: Christian Institute for the Study of Religion and Society, 1964), pp. 179-193 (revised

slightly from version published in *The Ecumenical Review* 14 [1961-62]: 154-163). The Institute, "CISRS," has also published other essays, sermons, and Bible studies of his; a bibliography appears in *In Memory of Devanandan* (1962).

86. London: Darton, Longman & Todd, 1964. The quotation cited at the end of the paragraph above is from p. 17. Boyd, *Indian . . .Theology* (cited above, note 75), pp. 222-226, has a brief treatment of this theologian who is currently perhaps the most significant in Hindu-Christian theological rapprochement, though the work of Fr. Klaus K. Klostermaier is also important; cf. the latter's *Kristvidya: A Sketch of an Indian Christology* (Indian Christian Thought Series, 8; Bangalore: Christian Institute for the Study of Religion and Society, 1967), and *Hindu and Christian in Vrindaban* (London: SCM, 1969).

87. *Colossians* (cited above, note 53), p. 60, note 211.

88. *Interpretation* 26 (1972): 328-337.

89. *Ibid.*, pp. 334f.

90. *Ibid.*, p. 335.

91. Cf. Sanders, *Christological Hymns* (cited above, note 59), pp. 9-12, 58-74, where some of the extensive literature is cited.

III: CREATION CONTINUES – REDEMPTIVELY

1. Cf. Anderson, *Creation Versus Chaos* (cited above, Chap. II, note 3), pp. 58-60, where it is argued that northern traditions generally, including D (the Deuteronomic history) and the prophets in the Northern Kingdom, as well as E, softpedaled the creation theme, thus remaining faithful to the central emphases in salvation history, i.e., Israel's rescue in the exodus and her election by Yahweh.

2. Examples are given in Sections A and B below.

3. For these creation stories, see the literature cited above in Chap. II, note 6, and in addition, for Greek thought, cf. Arnold Ehrhardt, *The Beginning: A Study in the Greek Philosophical Approach to the Concept of Creation from Anaximander to St John* (New York: Barnes & Noble, 1968).

4. See above, Chap. I, p. 7 and note 2.

5. The hymn which stands behind John 1:1-18, as it has been edited and used by the Fourth Evangelist, has been variously interpreted to mention the coming of the Logos, Jesus, for his earthly ministry either in v. 9 ("the true light . . . was coming into the world") or in v. 14 ("the Word became flesh"). Cf. Raymond E. Brown, S.S., *The Gospel According to John*, Vol. 1 (Anchor Bible, 29; Garden City, New York, 1966), pp. 3-37.

6. Cf. Philip B. Harner, "Creation Faith in Deutero-Isaiah," *Vetus Testamentum* 17 (1967): 298-306.

7. Cf. J. Philip Hyatt, "Was Yahweh Originally a Creator Deity?" *Journal of Biblical Literature* 86 (1967): 369-377, B. W. Anderson, "God, Names of," *Interpreter's Dictionary of the Bible* (cited above, Chap. II, note 29), Vol. 2, p. 410; and Anderson, *Creation Versus Chaos* (cited above, Chap. II, note 3), pp. 51f.

8. Cf. Anderson, *Creation Versus Chaos* (cited above, Chap. II, note 3), pp. 29-32, 39f., and passim.

9. See above, Chap. II, note 40.

10. Examples are given in Sections A and B below.

11. "The Theological Problem of ... Creation" (cited above, Chap. II, note 32), p. 142.

12. E.g., Rolf Rendtorff, "Die theologische Stellung des Schöpfungsglaubens bei Deuterojesaja, *Zeitschrift für Theologie und Kirche* 51 (1954): 3-13; and most pupils and scholars influenced by von Rad's view of salvation history.

13. E.g., Harner, "Creation Faith" (cited above, note 6); cf. B.D. Napier, "On Creation Faith in the Old Testament," *Interpretation* 16 (1962): 21-42.

14. "The Theology of Creation in the Old and New Testaments," in *The Root of the Vine* (festschrift for Anton Fridrichsen; London: Dacre Press, 1953), pp. 1-22; and Lindeskog's major monograph (of which only the first volume has appeared), *Studien zum neutestamentlichen Schöpfungsgedanken I* (Uppsala Universitets Arsskrift 1952:11; Uppsala: A. B. Lundequistska Bokhandeln, 1952).

15. Cf. A. D. Matthews, "The Prophetic Doctrine of Creation," *Church Quarterly Review* 166 (1965): 141-149. I have also profited in this area from conversations with my colleague, Dr. Foster R. McCurley Jr., whose unpublished S.T.M. dissertation (Philadelphia, 1964) dealt with "Creation Imagery and the Old Testament Prophets."

16. Cf. Anderson, *Creation Versus Chaos* (cited above, Chap. II, note 3), pp. 24-26; the section by Cyrus Gordon on Ugaritic materials in S. Kramer, *Mythologies* (cited above, Chap. I., note 6); and Loren R. Fisher, "Creation at Ugarit and in the Old Testament," *Vetus Testamentum* 15 (1965): 313-324.

17. H. W. Wolff, *Dodekapropheton 2, Joel und Amos* (Biblischer Kommentar Altes Testament XIV/2; Neukirchen-Vluyn: Neukirchener Verlag, 1969), pp. 254-256.

18. Anderson, *Creation Versus Chaos* (cited above, Chap. II, note 3), pp. 20f.; text in Pritchard, *Ancient Near Eastern Texts* (cited above, Chap. II, note 6), pp. 67f. (Tablet IV, lines 135ff.).

19. On the psalms generally, cf. the standard commentaries and Helmer Ringgren, *The Faith of the Psalmists* (Philadelphia: Fortress, and London: SCM, 1963).

20. Cf. above, Chap. II, pp. 33f., especially note 31.

21. Cf. the literature cited above, Chap. II, note 40.

22. "Creation, Cultus, and Faith in the Psalter," in *Horizons of Theological Education: Essays in Honor of Charles L. Taylor* (Dayton, Ohio: Association of Theological Schools 1966) (= *Theological Education* 2 [1966]), pp. 116-128.

23. *Ibid.*, p. 120.

24. Cf. commentaries; e.g., Toombs in *The Interpreter's One-Volume Commentary on the Bible* (cited above, Chap. II, note 31), on Psalm 19.

25. Christoph Barth, *Introduction to the Psalms* (New York: Scribner's, 1966), p. 60.

26. Ringgren, *Faith of the Psalmists* (cited above, note 19), pp. 96f.

27. *Old Testament Theology* (cited above, Chap. II, note 3), Vol. 1, p. 361.

28. So Harner, "Creation Faith" (cited above, note 6).

29. So Rendtorff, ". . .Schöpfungsglaubens . . ." (cited above, note 12); cf. Napier, "On Creation Faith . . ." (cited above, note 13).

30. Carroll Stuhlmueller, C.P., *Creative Redemption in Deutero-Isaiah* (Analecta Biblica, 43; Rome: Biblical Institute, 1970). This dissertation supercedes his earlier articles, while also building upon them, "The Theology of Creation in Second Isaias," *Catholic Biblical Quarterly* 21 (1959): 429-467; and " 'First and Last' and 'Yahweh-Creator' in Deutero-Isaiah," *ibid.*, 29 (1967): 495-511.

31. "The Theological Problem of . . . Creation" (cited above, Chap. II, note 32).

32. Rendtorff, ". . . Schöpfungsglaubens . . ." (cited above, note 12).

33. By Harner, whose article "Creation Faith" (cited above, note 6) and general position are summarized in the following two paragraphs.

34. Cited above, note 30, Stuhlmueller's views in *Creative Redemption* are in part sketched in the four paragraphs below.

35. *Ibid.*, p. 9 (italics omitted), cf. p. 233.

36. Isaiah 45:8, "Shower, O heavens, from above,
    and let the skies rain down righteousness;
    let the earth open, that salvation may sprout forth,
    and let it cause righteousness to spring up also;
    I the Lord have created it."

may specifically reflect the ancient Near Eastern imagery of the sky-god and his rain impregnating the open earth. The imagery from Israel's neighbors is relatively unrevised here by Israelite faith, though Yahweh is the one credited with this, and it is his "righteousness" which thus descends and springs up.

37. The phrase is attributed to Hartmut Gese.

38. Compare the analysis in the recent, standard commentaries on Isaiah 56-66.

39. On the characteristics of apocalyptic, cf. D. S. Russell, *The*

Method and Message of Jewish Apocalyptic (Philadelphia: Westminster, and London: SCM, 1964), pp. 104-139. In general, apocalyptic writings arise and the apocalyptic outlook is in vogue during dark and difficult times, when things are considered so bad that only a divine intervention will correct them; hence there is an effort to predict the future and foresee what will occur, and even when. But the message is usually in written (not spoken) form employing all sorts of symbols, and often adopts the name, pseudonymously, of some figure of the past. There is regularly hope expressed for some sort of life after death, given by God.

40. The reconstruction of the text followed here as to its sequence and division into units is that suggested by recent commentators. Cf. the treatment in Claus Westermann, *Isaiah 40-66: A Commentary*, trans. by D. M. G. Stalker (The Old Testament Library; London: SCM, and Philadelphia: Westminster, 1969), pp. 406-411.

41. The phrase "The 'Last Times' are like the 'First Times'" was developed by Hermann Gunkel in his book *Schöpfung und Chaos in Urzeit und Endzeit* (Göttingen: Vandenhoeck & Ruprecht, 1896; 2nd ed. 1921), and is discussed among other places in Claus Westermann, *Beginning and End in the Bible*, trans. by Keith Crim (Facet Books, Biblical Series, 31; Philadelphia: Fortress, 1972).

42. The prose or poetic nature of different sections of chapter 66 is one clue for analyzing it into component units from various hands; see the recent commentaries.

IV: NEW CREATION – HOPE AND NEW EXISTENCE NOW

1. For a survey of how many ways the adjective is used, besides the obvious application to the "new covenant (testament)" and examples noted below, cf. Roy A. Harrisville, "The Concept of Newness in the New Testament," *Journal of Biblical Literature* 74 (1955): 69-79; and his more detailed study, *The Concept of Newness in the New Testament* (Augsburg Theological Monographs; Minneapolis: Augsburg, 1960).

2. See above, Chap. II, Section A (pp. 24-31); the Excursus (pp. 42-56); and pp. 45, 58 (Heb. 1:2-3) and 45, 60 (John 1). A brief survey on "The New Testament Doctrine of *ktisis*" is provided by G. W. H. Lampe in the *Scottish Journal of Theology* 17 (1964): 449-462.

3. Cf. Bultmann, *Theology of the New Testament* (cited above, Chap. I, note 23), Vol. 1, pp. 69ff.; Kelly, *Early Christian Creeds* (cited above, Chap. II, note 10), pp. 12-29.

4. Cf. Russell, *Jewish Apocalyptic* (cited above, Chap. III, note 39), pp. 280-284; and the treatment of the Intertestamental literature in Lindeskog, *Studien* (cited above, Chap. III, note 14), pp. 85-134.

5. Space does not permit much discussion of or even listing of the

extensive literature about Jesus' expectations of the future, proposed
since Albert Schweitzer argued that Jesus was completely eschatological
in his outlook, expecting the Son-of-man figure to come on the clouds
of heaven even before his disciples had completed a preaching tour
throughout the little land of Palestine (Matt. 10:23) or, that failing,
upon his own death in Jerusalem. Some, like John A. T. Robinson, *Jesus
and His Coming* (Nashville & New York: Abingdon, and London: SCM,
1957), have tried to rescue Jesus from all such erroneous opinions about
the end by claiming that the references to a second coming stem from
the early church, not Jesus. Others (Bultmann and his pupils) see the
key in a distinction made by Jesus between himself and the coming Son
of man in verses like Mark 8:38. The traditional view is, of course, that
Jesus was always, and so understood himself as, the Son of man; but
when, then, did he expect the parousia to be? Paul's precise expectations
about the second coming and when it would be are likewise debated;
e.g., did he, as R. H. Charles (see note 17, below) and C. H. Dodd
suggest, develop a theology late in life which discarded the parousia, or
did he always regard a future eschatological fulfillment as essential
(Günther Bornkamm)? Johannine Christianity has been interpreted as
primarily oriented to present fulfillment and "eternal life" now, though
some passages (all of them, Bultmann thinks, from a later churchly editor)
point to a future side.

6. Cf. Ernst Käsemann, "The Beginnings of Christian Theology" and
"On the Topic of Primitive Christian Apologetic," Eng. trans. in *Apocalypticism* (cited above, Chap. I, note 26), pp. 17-46 and 99-133; and in
Käsemann's *New Testament Questions of Today*, trans. by W. J. Montague (Philadelphia: Fortress, and London: SCM, 1969), pp. 82-107 and
108-137.

7. Ethelbert Stauffer, among others, in his *New Testament Theology*,
trans. by John Marsh (London: SCM, and New York: Macmillan, 1955),
especially pp. 20f., sees apocalyptic as the clue to the way early Christians interpreted the Hebrew scriptures.

8. The phrase is used by John G. Gager Jr., "Functional Diversity in
Paul's Use of End-Time Language," *Journal of Biblical Literature* 89
(1970): 325-337.

9. Cf. the comments on apocalyptic above, Chap. III, note 39, and
almost any commentary on Revelation, e.g., Ronald H. Preston and
Anthony T. Hanson, *The Revelation of Saint John the Divine: Introduction and Commentary* (Torch Bible Commentaries; London: SCM, 1949),
pp. 15-17.

10. We follow the analysis of R. H. Charles in *A Critical and Exegetical Commentary on the Revelation of St. John*, 2 vols. (International
Critical Commentary series; Edinburgh; T. & T. Clark, 1920, reprinted
1959), Vol. 2, pp. 200-211, 376-378, and 443f.

11. Cf. George B. Caird, *A Commentary on the Revelation of St. John*

the Divine (Harper's/Black's New Testament Commentaries; London: A. & C. Black, New York: Harper & Row, 1966), pp. 261-266, 280.

12. So Eduard Lohse, *Die Offenbarung des Johannes* (Das Neue Testament Deutsch; Göttingen: Vandenhoeck & Ruprecht, 1966), p. 104.

13. Many recent commentaries and some of the older ones abandon the tradition of authorship by Peter himself and date 2 Peter as late as A.D. 150. Cf. E. Käsemann, "An Apologia for Primitive Christian Eschatology," in *New Testament Essays*, trans. by W. J. Montague (Studies in Biblical Theology, 41; London: SCM, and Naperville: Allenson, 1964), pp. 169-195.

14. Cf. J. Reumann and W. H. Lazareth, *Righteousness and Society: Ecumenical Dialog in a Revolutionary Age* (Philadelphia: Fortress, 1967), pp. 91f.

15. It may be suggested that use in 2 Peter 3 of the phrase "new heavens and new earth" parallels that in Isaiah 66, and the usage in Revelation 21 is more like that in Isaiah 65.

16. An exception is D. E. H. Whiteley, *The Theology of St. Paul* (Oxford: Basil Blackwell, and Philadelphia: Fortress, 1964), who treats "Creation" and "The 'Supernatural' Creation," pp. 17-44.

17. Cf. note 5 above. This is to decide against the scheme of four stages in Paul's "developing thought" from "crude" Jewish apocalyptic to "mature" theology which no longer talks of future fulfillment but sees Christ's cosmic significance now, proposed by R. H. Charles, *Eschatology: A Critical History of the Doctrine of a Future Life* (London: A. & C. Black, 1899, cited from the 2d ed. 1913; reprinted, with an Introduction by G. W. Buchanan, New York: Schocken Books, 1963), pp. 437-463, a pattern of supposed development endorsed by many scholars; and to agree with Käsemann and others that Paul's genuine writings always exhibit a "future reservation" — all is not yet fulfilled and some aspects are reserved for the future, cf. Käsemann's "On . . . Primitive Christian Apocalyptic" (cited above, note 6), pp. 118-133, especially 132 (in *New Testament Questions*, pp. 108-137, especially 136).

18. The phrase is especially used by Lindeskog (cited above, Chap. III, note 14).

19. See Lindeskog, especially *Studien* (cited above, Chap. III, note 14).

20. Cf. Ehrhardt, *The Beginning* (cited above, Chap. III, note 3).

21. See above, Chap. II, Section A, pp. 24-31; we assume that neither the hymn at Col. 1:15-20 nor the Colossian epistle is by Paul himself.

22. Sin, as a theme and problem, reappears in Paul with an emphasis and intensity seldom found since the J writer, save in late Jewish apocalyptic; cf. above, Chap. II, p. 34, and note 34.

23. Cited above, note 1.

24. The following renderings indicate the diversity of interpretation at 2 Cor. 5:17: KJV, "he is a new creature"; NEB, "there is a new world"; "he is a new being" (Twentieth Century New Testament); "he becomes a new person altogether" (J. B. Phillips).

25. *A Greek-English Lexicon of the New Testament and Other Early Christian Literature*, by Walter Bauer, trans. by W. F. Arndt and F. W. Gingrich (New York: Cambridge University Press, and Chicago: University of Chicago Press, 1957), under its entry *"ktisis."*

26. New York: Pageant Press, 1958. Cf. the review in the *Journal of Biblical Literature* 79 (1960): 387f.

27. In the series Aufsätze und Vorträge zur Theologie und Religionswissenschaft 25 (Berlin: Evangelische Verlag, 1963). Also, subtitled *Ein Beitrag zum Verständnis der Auferweckung bei Paulus*, in the series Arbeiten zur Theologie, I. Reihe, Heft 12 (Stuttgart: Calwer Verlag, 1963). On alternate interpretations of Schwantes' key phrase at Romans 4:17, cf. W. Sanday and A. C. Headlam, *A Critical and Exegetical Commentary on the Epistle to the Romans*, International Critical Commentary series (Edinburgh: T. & T. Clark, 5th ed. 1902), pp. 113f.; they interpret it to mean "issue His summons to generations yet unborn."

28. Cited above, Chap. I, note 29.

29. Cf. Galloway, *The Cosmic Christ* (cited above, Chap. II, note 63) and the literature mentioned in Chap. I, pp. 14ff., and in the Excursus, pp. 42ff.

30. Cf. above, pp. 16, 59f.

31. This has been remarked by reviewers of *Creation and Redemption;* cf. above, Chap. II, note 19. The very term "lord" (lordship) already had a varied series of meanings prior to Paul; cf. W. Kramer, *Christ, Lord, Son of God* (cited above, Chap. II, note 8).

32. "Die Idee der Neuschöpfung beim Apostel Paulus und ihr religionsgeschichtlicher Hintergrund," *Trier Theologische Zeitschrift* 68 (1959): 257-270; and his book, *Kaine Ktisis* (Trier, 1959).

33. Ernest De Witt Burton, *A Critical and Exegetical Commentary on the Epistle to the Galatians* (International Critical Commentary series; Edinburgh: T. & T. Clark, 1921), p. 355.

34. *Saint Paul's Epistle to the Galatians* (London: Macmillan, 10th rev. ed., 1890), p. 224.

35. W. D. Davies, *Paul and Rabbinic Judaism: Some Rabbinic Elements in Pauline Theology* (London: SPCK, 1948, reprinted 1964), pp. 119-121. Joachim Jeremias, *Infant Baptism in the First Four Centuries*, trans. by David Cairns (Philadelphia: Westminster, 1960), pp. 29ff., especially 33 and 36.

36. This is so because rabbinic material was transmitted orally for some time and only later written down. Thus, written records are late,

but presumably material goes back much earlier. The investigator must try to establish the likelihood that a tradition written down only in a later Christian century actually goes back prior to the fall of Jerusalem in A.D. 70 or to the time of Jesus or pre-Christian decades. Form-critical investigation of rabbinic materials is only beginning, pioneered by Jacob Neusner among others.

37. A certain caution must be urged in the use of such documents as those cited from the Pseudepigrapha above, since 2 Baruch is to be dated around A.D. 100 (but likely made up from earlier sources) and the library of materials that makes up 1 (or Ethiopic) Enoch, while usually dated in the second or first century B.C., now seems to include some sections crucial for the study of Christian origins (chapters 37-71) which, judged in the light of Qumran finds to date, seem to be from the Christian period or even the second century A.D. (J. T. Milik).

38. "Erwägungen zum ontologischen Charakter der *kainē ktisis* bei Paulus," *Evangelische Theologie* 27 (1967): 1-35.

39. It is possible that Christian use of *Kainē ktisis,* in the sense of "new creation" (of the whole cosmos), arose as a slogan among Hellenistic Christian enthusiasts of the sort who gave us the hymns today discoverable at Colossians 1:15-20, 1 Timothy 3:16, Philippians 2:6-11, and elsewhere, passages where Christ's lordship is extended by acclamation to the entire cosmos.

40. So Stuhlmacher, cited above, note 38.

41. Observed by Johannes Weiss, in his commentary, *Der erste Korintherbrief,* Meyer Kritisch-Exegetischer Kommentar (Göttingen: Vandenhoek & Ruprecht, 10. Auflage 1925), p. 186.

42. Cf. Günther Bornkamm, "Baptism and New Life in Paul" (1939), Eng. trans. by Paul L. Hammer in Bornkamm's collected essays, *Early Christian Experience* (New York: Harper & Row, 1969), pp. 71-86.

43. Cited above, note 38.

44. So Gager (cited above, note 8); and Anton Vögtle, "Röm 8, 19-22: eine schöpfungs-theologische oder anthropologische-soteriologische Aussage?" in *Mélanges Bibliques en hommage au R.P. Béda Rigaux* (Gembloux, Belgium: Duculot, 1970), pp. 351-366, and in his volume, *Das Neue Testament und die Zukunft des Kosmos* (Düsseldorf: Patmos-Verlag, 1970), pp. 183-207. On the principle, cf. W. Grundmann, "Überlieferung und Eigenaussage im eschatologischen Denken des Apostels Paulus," *New Testament Studies* 8 (1961-62): 12-26. Cf. also, however, Horst R. Balz, *Heilsvertrauen und Welterfahrung: Strukturen der paulinischen Eschatologie nach Römer 8, 18-39* (Beiträge zur evangelische Theologie, 59; Munich: Christian Kaiser, 1971), reviewed by John G. Gibbs in the *Journal of Biblical Literature* 91 (1972): 268f.

45. In the materials which are cited above in note 44.

V: SOME CONCLUSIONS ABOUT CREATION
AND NEW CREATION

1. *The Human Crisis in Ecology* (cited above, Chap. I, note 1), pp. 101f.

2. See above, pp. 59-61, with the qualifications and possibilities indicated there. I am conscious of one major area not treated in these chapters where an interest in creation could have existed apart from any stress on redemption, namely, the wisdom literature and tradition. This area of ancient Near Eastern and New Testament thinking deserves fuller treatment than a footnote allows, and it is one matter to which the examples selected above do not do justice. In part, however, the question here is not simply how "creation" in wisdom literature relates to redemption but how wisdom as a whole is understood in relation to Israelite or early Christian faith.

3. *Creation and Redemption* (cited above, Chap. I, note 29).

4. See above, p. 30.

5. See above, pp. 18 and 30f.

6. So Joachim Jeremias, *Jesus' Promise to the Nations*, trans. by S. H. Hooke (Studies in Biblical Theology, 24; London: SCM, and Naperville: Allenson, 1958, 2d ed., 1967); and his *New Testament Theology: Part One, The Proclamation of Jesus* (London: SCM, and New York: Scribner's, 1971), pp. 245-47.

7. So Karl Rahner and others; cf. above, pp. 14f., 42ff., for literature reflecting this view.

8. See above, pp. 46f., and the titles by Schweizer given in Chap. II, note 68.

9. Cf. Chap. I, above, pp. 10f.